Praise for
Free to Love, Free to H ̶ ̶ ̶

"Love is the essence of healing. Healing is th̶ ̶ ̶ ̶ ̶ ̶ ̶ove. In this beautiful book, my friend and colleague Dr. David Simon lovingly shares the essential truths about love and healing. With his guidance, you will be able to open your heart and heal your body."

— **Deepak Chopra, M.D.,** Chopra Center co-founder and author of *Spiritual Solutions*

"David Simon is a unique treasure, a rare combination of medical doctor and spiritual healer. He has blessed my life in both capacities, and I am delighted to be able to recommend him to others."

— **Marianne Williamson,** author of *Return to Love*

"Years ago, a pediatric surgeon, Dr. Bernie Siegel, wrote, 'A fundamental problem most patients face is the inability to love themselves.' Truer words were never spoken. In *Free to Love, Free to Heal,* physician David Simon teaches you step-by-step precisely how to experience the unparalleled healing power of self-love and self-acceptance. This is a book for all of us."

— **Christiane Northrup, M.D.,** author of *Women's Bodies, Women's Wisdom*

"Dr. David Simon is the world grand master of medical practice based on new paradigm physiology, where emotions are understood as the molecular basis of thought, health and disease. Dr. Simon has helped thousands of patients with his powerful combination of ancient teachings and modern science. Now the pioneer of mind-body medicine has written a very wise book for us all. *Free to Love, Free to Heal* gives us advanced yet simple tools to erase the past hurts that diminish our happiness, allowing us to live in gratitude from the heart."

— **Candace Pert, PhD.,** neuroscientist and author of *Molecules of Emotion*

"This brilliant and compelling book is a balm for the wounded heart, offering you a genuine awakening to your own authentic nature. If you follow Dr. David Simon's wise and loving approach, you'll have an experience of unconditional self-acceptance and an expansion of healing and joy in every aspect of your life. He has been my most trusted teacher and I know you can be transformed under his guidance."

— **Debbie Ford,** author of *Courage: Overcoming Fear and Igniting Self-Confidence*

"This is a wonderful book to heal emotional toxicity, release pain, and forge a path to love – an important journey to freedom and awakening."

— **Judith Orloff, M.D.,** author of *Emotional Freedom*

"Dr. Simon is superbly trained in medicine and wonderfully sensitive to the Human Spirit. This rare combination gives him a remarkable insight into the multitude of ailments that pursue most modern people. With this ability he calls on the best of our modern medical skills and also a wealth of traditional treatments of the Orient. *Free to Love, Free to Heal* is a treasury of insights into our modern world and a guide to the alleviation of its suffering."

— **Robert A. Johnson,** Jungian analyst and author of *He, She, We,* and *Inner Work.*

Free to
Love
Free to
Heal

Also by David Simon, M.D.

Books

The Seven Spiritual Laws of Yoga Guidebook

Vital Energy: The 7 Keys to Invigorate Body, Mind and Soul

The 10 Commitments: Translating Good Intentions into Great Choices

*Return to Wholeness: Embracing Body, Mind and Spirit
in the Face of Cancer*

*The Wisdom of Healing: A Natural Mind Body Program
for Optimal Wellness*

*Grow Younger, Live Longer: 10 Steps to Reverse Aging
(with Deepak Chopra)*

*Freedom from Addiction: The Chopra Center Method for Overcoming
Destructive Habits (with Deepak Chopra)*

*The Chopra Center Herbal Guide: 40 Prescriptions for Perfect Health
(with Deepak Chopra)*

*Magical Beginnings, Enchanted Lives: A Holistic Guide to Pregnancy
and Childbirth (with Deepak Chopra)*

*

All of the above are available at your local bookstore
store.chopra.com.

Free to
Love
Free to
Heal

Heal Your Body by Healing Your Emotions

David Simon, M.D.

CHOPRA CENTER PRESS

WWW.CHOPRA.COM

Published by Chopra Center Press, a division of Chopra Enterprises, L.L.C., 2013 Costa del Mar Road, Carlsbad, California 92009
www.chopra.com

Originally published in hardcover by Chopra Center Press in 2009.

Printed in the United States of America

Design by Lubosh Cech
okodesignstudio.com

Photography by Aaron Dressin
aarondressin.com

ISBN 978-0-9819640-1-0
Revised edition.

Permission to use poetry translations provided by Daniel Ladinsky.
Complete poems are published in:
The Gift, Penguin Compass, 1999, NY, NY;
Love Poems from God, Penguin Compass, 2002, NY, NY;
I Heard God Laughing, Penguin Books, 2006, NY, NY.

The information contained in this book is not intended as a substitute for appropriate or necessary professional medical or psychological care.
Please review any approaches you are considering implementing into your life with your trusted health-care provider.

To the sacred lovers,
Whose essence is healing.
To the sacred healers,
Whose essence is loving.

Acknowledgments

My unbounded gratitude flows to the many loving hearts that contributed to the birthing of this book.

To my beloved partner in love, Pam, and to my beautiful mirrors of love, Max, Sara, and Isabel;

To the precious beings who taught me my earliest lessons in love, Lee Shirley, Myron, Ethel, Sarah, Jill, and Howard;

To Kyla Stinnett for her impeccable commitment to clarity, and to Brookes Nohlgren for her invaluable refinements;

To Lynn Franklin and her talented team for their dedication to seeing these words reach a global audience;

To the Chopra Center Press tribe, David Greenspan, Tiffany Murray, Erika DeSimone, Sara Harvey, Asha MacIsaac, Vijay Singh, and Charley Paz for their selfless attention, energy, and creativity;

To Amanda Ringnalda, Trista Thorp, Dave Goodley, and Janis Steiner for creating and holding the space that enables us to explore these heart healing principles;

To my dear friends and teachers, Deepak Chopra, Debbie Ford, Marshall Rosenberg, and Robert Johnson for expanding my vocabulary of love;
To Daniel Ladinsky for his gracious permission to share the sacred heart of Hafiz and other beings of light with my readers;

And to Lubosh Cech for his magnificent talent in manifesting this book.

Contents

Preface

I STILL VIVIDLY REMEMBER MY EXPERIENCES AS A MEDICAL STUDENT delivering babies on the South Side of Chicago. After hours of intense labor there finally arrived that precious moment of immense relief and joy when a newborn was embraced by its mother, and the world took a deep breath. Regardless of the drama or circumstances heralding the birth, the pure sweet potential of a new life was palpable. As Carl Sandburg said, "A baby is God's opinion that life should go on."

Every life is sacred. You arrived in this world innocent and open, with the unequivocal expectation for unconditional love. It may have taken months or even years for the idea to emerge that you actually had to *do* something other than exist to deserve love. After incubating for nine months in a sea of unity, you required some time to see yourself as a separate being.

But sooner or later you did. You learned to compartmentalize and prioritize, concealing parts of yourself that received negative feedback while refining those aspects of your nature that generated positive responses. You learned which of your actions evoked approval and which brought upset, gradually molding yourself into a personality with the hope of recapturing the unconditional loving you carry as a memory in the heart of your being. For the fortunate ones, this path back to love is relatively uncomplicated; but for many, it is strewn with obstacles. Challenging family dynamics, sibling rivalries, physical health concerns, disruptive household moves, awkward relationships, and difficulties at school are just a few of the encumbrances that cause people to doubt they are unconditionally lovable.

This belief of unlovability manifests in many disguises. It may appear as obesity or anorexia, depression or anxiety, allergies or autoimmune disorders. Digestive problems, chronic pain, and fatigue can all reflect underlying emotional malnourishment.

I wrote *Free to Love, Free to Heal* as a guide to help you identify and release the impediments to your ability to give and receive love. This book will show you how to recognize the parts within you that hurt and apply the balm of loving to promote emotional and physical healing.

I recently met with a woman, Elizabeth, who illustrates how our stories shape our emotional and physical health. She suffered from depression for years, and her chronic fatigue and recurrent migraines severely limited her activities. Elizabeth carried a handful of painful memories associated with her mother, who was eventually diagnosed with bipolar disorder. In one, she recalled her mother saying in a moment of anger that Elizabeth was an accident and the only reason she remained in a loveless marriage. In another, she overheard her mother in a heated argument with her father, referring to Elizabeth as a parasite who was draining her life. Although her parents remain in their conflict-ridden marriage to this day, she still carries the sense that she is to blame for their unhappiness, and more importantly, she cannot shake the feeling of being unwanted and unworthy. She had woven these memories and her childhood interpretations into a story that contributed to her chronic health challenges and sabotaged her ability to love and be loved.

While acknowledging our wounds and expressing our feelings of hurt and fear is fundamental to healing them, life is too short to allow the violations, losses, misunderstandings, distortions, and disappointments of the past to dictate our course moving forward. We are innately creative beings capable of writing a love story worth living, and we cannot afford to miss out on the opportunity to experience nourishing relationships. If we are willing to shed the constricting skin that keeps us from knowing our true nature, we can recapture our birthright as beings of love. It is to this end that I welcome you on this journey to emotional freedom, which is at the heart of true healing.

Introduction

How We Heal

Love has no opposite. Love has no conflict.

— J. KRISHNAMURTI

IN MY ROLE AS A "MIND-BODY" PHYSICIAN, I HEAR MANY HEART-RENDING tales. Over the three decades I've been practicing medicine, I've come to see a person's migraines, fatigue, digestive distress, or back pain as a kind of admission pass that entitles the bearer to a few moments of a doctor's attention. After listening to people's problems for so many years, I've learned that when I can create enough safety for the sufferer, an underlying story – a story that at its heart is about giving or receiving love – will be revealed to me. And if I as a doctor can coax the hidden meaning of the illness into the open, then healing can begin.

As you may have guessed, seeking the emotional roots of a patient's illness is not something I picked up in medical school. On the contrary, my conventional medical training taught me that my responsibility is to relieve symptoms: Prescribe a pain reliever to subdue a headache; add an acid blocker to extinguish heartburn; sprinkle on a selective serotonin reuptake inhibitor to alleviate depression. In this era of managed care, in which one out of four doctor visits lasts less than ten minutes, providing symptomatic relief for a person's distress is a practical and worthy endeavor.

An anti-anxiety medicine may not get to the root of your problem, but it will help you feel less stressed during the day. An anti-inflammatory drug may not address the core issues underlying your chronic pain, but it should enable you to do housework with a little less discomfort. And if you develop indigestion as a result of your daily doses of pain medicine, a potent antacid will soothe your stomach. There is indisputable value in lessening the symptoms of distress, and it is not my intention to disparage any approach that relieves the suffering of humanity.

Still, long before beginning medical school I sensed that illness presents a deeper opportunity for healing and transformation, which we miss when we focus on symptom relief. Like a young child, the body communicates its needs in a relatively simple and straightforward manner. Whether it wants nourishment, affection, new experiences, time to rest, or a chance to release toxins, your body generates sensations to get attention. When you listen to these signals and address the basic needs they represent, your body responds by producing chemicals of comfort. When you fail to heed your body's message, its calls become louder. If despite its best efforts your body is unable to get your attention, it may stop talking for a while, but when next heard from, it will not be ignored.

Hearing Your Story

Most of us have a story underlying why we become ill. In the businessman's mind, his heart attack is the result of relentless job stress that offers overwhelming pressure but little appreciation at work and at home. To the recently divorced woman, her irritable bowel syndrome is the culmination of years of unwillingness to listen to her gut feelings and leave an abusive relationship. The adult child of an alcoholic parent senses that her chronic weight problem somehow protects her from the pain of early emotional abuse.

Our reductionistic medical science resists these connections. Heart-burn results not from job stress, but from hydrochloric acid molecules leaking into the esophagus. High blood pressure is caused by excessive amounts of circulating angiotensin molecules, not a turbulent marriage. Your insomnia has little to do with the early childhood experience of your parents arguing after you went to bed; rather, it reflects a deficiency of the inhibitory neurotransmitter GABA. Your depression is explain-able by a lack of serotonin, so there is no need to explore whether your relationships are nurturing or if you're fulfilling your true life purpose. Though in each case the symptom has its roots in an underlying narrative about the inability to give or receive love, in conventional medicine we continue to ignore the love story that longs to be revealed.

People as Molecules

It took me most of my years in medical school to grasp the mind-set that drives our conventional approach to physical and emotional distress. The biological sciences teach us that people are biochemical bags. If you accept this basic assumption, it logically follows that the best treatment for most disorders is a pharmaceutical.

Drugs are effective. With them, I can (at least for a while) put you to sleep, wake you up, slow or accelerate the movement of food through your digestive tract, raise or lower your blood pressure, and numb your pain. The downside, of course, is that if a medication is effective, you are not required to examine your life or change the way you live. And yet it is in these self-examinations and positive life changes that the key to healing lies.

Your Body Is Trying to Tell You Something

We often miss the signals our body is sending until we suffer. After an argument with your spouse, you wolf down several slices of leftover pepperoni pizza right before bed. You awaken an hour later with terrible heartburn, but within fifteen minutes of chewing a couple of antacid tablets, your indigestion subsides. What have you learned? Although your body (and soul) might like you to consider how your emotional anguish translates into digestive distress, the only lesson you may have learned was to take your medicine *before* going to bed.

Since the discovery of penicillin in 1928, conventional medicine has been driven in a noble quest to find a silver bullet for every ailment. The pursuit of cures for cancer, arthritis, and Alzheimer's disease drives our medical research community, and we've witnessed important advances in our ability to alleviate suffering. Still, our power to solve the most pervasive health problems facing our society remains limited at best. If there were pills that could cure anxiety, alcoholism, obesity, or irritable bowel syndrome without significant side effects, there would be little reason not to take them. Sadly, there are few conditions causing human suffering that have surrendered to our "pill for every ill" approach. In the vast majority of cases, medicines lessen, but do not eliminate symptoms – and they often carry side effects that are as distressing, and at times as dangerous, as the illnesses for which they are prescribed.

An Alternative Alternative

So, what is the alternative? The word *alternative* still carries a lot of emotional charge for many in the healthcare field. From the perspective of conventional allopathic doctors, "alternative" implies unproven interventions that keep people from accepting effective care. For non-conventional health practitioners, alternative refers to individualized therapies that relieve "dis-ease," even if they have not been subjected to rigorous scientific scrutiny.

I have a different perspective. Although I embrace any approach that can provide relief to your body or mind, I'm wary of interventions that place the power in the hands of the healthcare practitioner, whether it be a medical doctor, chiropractor, or herbalist. I'm pleased when an acupuncture treatment, homeopathic remedy, or nutritional supplement eases someone's functional bowel disorder or headaches; yet, I wonder how long the reprieve can last if awareness and healing of the underlying mind-body turbulence do not accompany the relief – if the story or "biography" beneath the biology is not addressed. If a person does not learn to heal the deeper wound impeding their ability to give and receive love, another expression of the underlying story will emerge.

When a doctor "fixes" someone without exploring the context of the illness, the symptoms may abate but the unmet needs will persist, and the person's mental, emotional, and physical health will remain vulnerable. A migraine sufferer's headaches may be less intense with medication, but her insomnia becomes more troublesome. The pain relievers prescribed to reduce a lawyer's backache lead to an escalation of his digestive complaints. Pharmacologically suppressing a stay-at-home mom's anxiety shifts her focus to chronic fatigue. The body is trying to tell us something, but rather than hearing the message, conventional medicine's tendency is to use drugs as more effective sound barriers.

Keep the Baby, Learn Why It's Crying

There are, of course, times of crisis when appropriate medical interventions are necessary and lifesaving. If you fracture your arm in an automobile accident, you need a good orthopedic surgeon. If you develop bacterial bronchitis, you will most likely require antibiotics. If you develop a rapid heart rate, promptly get to the nearest emergency room to be evaluated by a cardiologist.

But even with accidents, infections, and arrhythmias there is almost always a love story waiting in the wings. Perhaps you were having a heated argument with your partner on your cell phone and ran a stop sign, prompting the collision that resulted in your bone injury. Maybe your bronchitis developed because you had secretly started smoking again after your most recent relationship dissolved. Perhaps your heart palpitations were triggered by the extra caffeine you've been consuming to override your exhaustion from staying awake at night wondering if you should remain in your marriage. Emotional pain binds our hearts and makes us sick. To regain genuine health, we must be free to love.

Responsibility, Not Blame

There is rarely a simple explanation for physical or emotional illness, and looking for the deeper story – the illness's subtext, if you will – does *not* mean assigning blame when your body becomes ill or your mind becomes distressed. Pursuing the answer to *why* people become ill is only of value if it leads to more productive thoughts, feelings, and behaviors. The last thing a suffering person needs is the additional burden of thinking that they caused their illness or could have prevented it if they had made other choices. Responsibility and blame are not the same. One uplifts and empowers, the other weakens and depletes.

A close friend of mine recently discovered that her cancer had recurred after being in remission for several years. Her first question to me was, "What did I do to bring this back?" Knowing her enthusiasm for life, her love for friends and family, and her overall healthy lifestyle, I could not support her self-flogging over being too ambitious or trying to manage too many projects. Even if it were true (which I do not believe), this type of inner dialogue is unproductive – it does nothing to improve the situation.

The essence of responsibility is recognizing that regardless of what has happened up until now, we are capable of making new choices that can improve our situation moving forward. We always have the *ability to respond* in creative ways that allow for something new to emerge.

Each week at the Chopra Center for Wellbeing, I see guests struggling with challenges that at times seem overwhelming. Serious physical or emotional issues are exhausting, but when people are willing to look at the story behind their illness (which ultimately is a story they have been telling to themselves), do the work of releasing the toxic emotions they've been carrying, and begin thinking and doing things differently, healing and transformation occur.

I have led thousands of people along this path to identifying and releasing feelings and beliefs that are not serving them. Having supervised people individually and in group settings, I know there is tremendous value in having an ally on your journey to emotional freedom. Still, because even in a group, individuals are on a journey of self-discovery, I believe it is possible to do this work on your own. Although finding a good counselor or life coach who approaches life from a holistic framework can be immeasurably helpful, doing this work with a trusted and devoted partner or friend can be similarly powerful. *Free to Love, Free to Heal* workshops may also be available in your community.

Throughout this book, I will provide safe guidelines designed to maximize the benefits of this process with minimal risk. You may feel some temporary emotional discomfort as previously concealed toxic beliefs and memories rise to your conscious awareness in preparation for being released. Make the commitment to follow this course of action through to its healing conclusion, and you will experience the exhilaration that comes from expanding the lightness of your being. Now let's get started plotting our path to freedom.

Chapter One

Growing Up Human

What keeps us alive, what allows us to endure?
I think it is the hope of loving, or being loved.

— MEISTER ECKHART

I OFTEN ASK MY PATIENTS STRUGGLING WITH A LIFE ISSUE, "DO YOU deserve to be happy?" More often than not, I receive a tenuous answer. "I'd like to say I do, but I'm not so sure" is a fairly typical response. Or I may hear, "I can't remember anyone in my life ever telling me it's my right to be happy." Well, if you haven't heard it before, hear it now: YOU DESERVE TO BE HAPPY!

Although relatively few of us were told during our upbringing that the expansion of happiness is *the* purpose of life, most people sense somewhere in their soul that more joy ought to be part of the equation. How, then, do we move from a state of constriction to a state of ever greater freedom and happiness? The first step towards genuine awakening is setting the intention . . . deciding to live a life that reflects your right to happiness. This requires the recognition that you have the capacity to change the plotline of your life, even if you've been acting from the same script since before you can remember. It requires the recognition that you are the only one who cares enough about your happiness to make it a driving force. It requires the recognition that unless you loosen the hold that your past has on you, your future will unfold in much the same way. It requires believing at the deepest level of your being that you are capable and deserving of love.

To reach this level of awareness, it can be helpful to recall how human beings become who we are. Each of us has a unique story to tell, and yet there are universal themes that shape all our lives. Let's explore the basic themes that define the human condition. Once you understand how you came to be who you are, you will be in a better position to become the person you want to be.

Incubation: Our First Nine Months

I have yet to meet a person who remembers choosing to incarnate. Although I can imagine a scenario in which a free-floating soul watches a couple having sex and decides, "I'm going to incarnate into that dysfunctional family," I do not know anyone who can honestly recall making that choice.

We therefore inexplicably find ourselves incubating in a womb in which we are entirely dependent upon the choices made by our mother. While we may have been wanted (though 50 percent of pregnancies are unplanned), pregnancy is more often than not a stressful experience for both the potential mother and father.

Day-to-day stresses of life affect everyone, and compounded with the perpetual hormonal shifts that pregnant mothers endure, it is likely that your nine months between conception and birth were not continuously idyllic. Although we might like to believe otherwise, few of us were genuinely incubated in joy.

Still, because of the high priority nature bestows upon embryonic forms, the basic necessities of a fetus are usually met without major interruption. In the womb there is no lag between the arising of a biological need and its fulfillment. A developing baby does not have to endure the discomforts of hunger, fatigue, or a full bladder. Psychiatrist Carl Jung called this a state of "unconscious perfection," which may persist for a few months after birth.

When after nine months we've outgrown our sheltered residence, we go through a cataclysmic eviction, which fortunately no one remembers. Soon after, we begin the process of creating a personality – of becoming a person.

Symbiosis: The Seeds of Self

Assuming our mother is reasonably available, in our first few months of life we have only a vague sense of separation or "other." In this stage, called *symbiosis,* our sense of being is inextricably entangled with our mother. If she is happy and comfortable, we are as well; if she's not, we're not. When she is attentive and devoted to us, our uncomfortable feelings of hunger magically manifest a breast or bottle and transform into pleasure. Our fatigue generates a gentle rocking until we're asleep. We release the pressure in our bladder and within moments the annoying wetness is removed as our diaper is changed.

Our sense of self at this stage is purely visceral. We *are* our physical sensations; we *are* our feelings. If our basic needs are met, we feel safe and comfortable. If, through no fault of our own, our mother is distracted, unavailable, or incapable of tuning in to our needs, our core sense of identity – which includes our lovability – is questioned, and we may have difficulty developing the trust that our discomfort will eventually resolve into comfort. These earliest experiences can influence the way we view ourselves as well as our ability to love for the rest of our life.

Self-Image: Learning Who We Are Through the Mirror of Relationship

Our primary caregivers provided continuous feedback as we achieved our developmental milestones – learning to sit, crawl, walk, and talk. If we had loving parents, they reinforced each accomplishment with praise and encouragement, while simultaneously setting appropriate boundaries that kept us safe. Being repeatedly told how adorable, clever, competent, and talented we were enabled us to develop the membrane of our self-image. With emotionally healthy, loving, mature caregivers, we were able to create a sense of self that integrated and reflected the approval and appreciation we received from those around us. We became aware that we were lovable.

If, however, our parents, burdened by their own wounding, distress, or exhaustion, were inconsistent in their nurturing feedback, we internalized their distortions. In our innocence, we failed to recognize that the distorted image was not a result of our flaws, but was caused by "defects" in the caregivers who served as our reflectors. We mistakenly assumed that our core self was wrong or unacceptable because we didn't receive the message that we were lovable and unconditionally loved. Our self-image – positive or negative – develops through the mirror of our relationships.

Self-Expansion

Children with a healthy self-image possess a baseline sense of well-being. They know they have intrinsic value and anticipate the world's acknowledgment of it. Once they've developed this sense of self-worth, they are able to progressively expand their boundaries through accomplishment, achievement, and nurturing relationships. With the guidance of compassionate parents and teachers, they define and refine their healthy sense of self throughout adolescence.

Without this core sense of value, children approach the world with trepidation, apprehension, and frustration. If caregivers are unable to fortify a child's healthy sense of self at this juncture, subsequent stages will most likely include friction-filled interactions with the world.

Boundary Testing

The teenage years are about testing limits – for both teenagers and their parents. Although boundary skirmishes with peers and authority figures are expected and ultimately healthy, few of us navigate this stage without some emotional bruising. Distinctions become potential liabilities. The concept of "too" becomes firmly established at this time – too fat/too skinny, too tall/too small, too smart/too slow. Our peers, classmates, and siblings may exploit any trait we have that deviates from the average, as a means of deflecting attention away from their own insecurities.

If they have successfully moved through earlier development stages, most teenagers are able to emerge from this boundary-testing period with a sense of self-worth, as well as a personal inventory of abilities and talents that they will continue to cultivate into adulthood. Some adolescents, however, get stuck at this stage, and essential components of personality remain undeveloped. For these individuals, weaknesses and vulnerabilities in self-esteem will likely persist, affecting their choices and experiences in all areas of life.

These formative experiences can have a persistent influence on a person's personality and health. For example, a girl who enters puberty early and is not taught how to manage the new attention she receives may become withdrawn and lose her confidence in herself. At a party, she discovers that drinking alcohol relieves her self-conscious discomfort and for the first time, she is able to enjoy being with others. Unfortunately, drinking in order to be sociable becomes a pattern that persists well into adulthood. In short, our inner sense of self informs and influences the reality we create for ourselves and our ability to give and receive love.

Ideal Parental Qualifications

Human beings are biologically capable of reproduction long before they are emotionally equipped for parenting. Isn't it ironic that a license is required to go fishing but not to have a child? It isn't surprising, then, that so many children are raised in environments where those in charge are learning on the job. Given the fact that pregnancies are so often unplanned (and the reality that even many of those parents who do plan for children are not emotionally qualified), we have to acknowledge that many of us were parented poorly and need to re-write our internal parental script.

In an ideal world, parents-to-be would have five key emotional characteristics, the possession of which would substantially increase the likelihood of their children developing a healthy sense of self. By exploring the ideal parental qualities, we can begin to cultivate these traits in ourselves – in the *internalized* parents who now reside in our own psyche. Healing our "inner parents" enhances our ability to love and our likelihood of becoming free to heal.

The five ideal parental traits are:

1) Self-awareness
2) Emotional availability
3) A vitality-enhancing lifestyle
4) Skillful conscious communication
5) Balanced boundary management

Self-Awareness

Parents who have not resolved their own emotional and psychological issues face a difficult challenge in supporting a child's healthy development. Again, in an ideal world, potential parents would ask themselves, *Am I happy with who I am? Do I love the person I am?* If the answers were anything but an authentic "yes," before taking on the responsibility for another being's healthy development and happiness, prospective parents would first engage in the inner work of identifying, moving through, and releasing the emotional residue that had built up inside them, inhibiting their ability to love.

Emotional Availability

Providing food and love are the primary duties of parents. Just as prospective parents must ask themselves if they have the financial resources to provide for a child's needs, potential mothers and fathers need to ask the question, *Do I have the internal resources to lovingly care for another human being?* Connecting with one's own feelings while resonating with another's is the essence of emotional intelligence. Only those capable of embracing the full range of human emotions without losing their sense of self are qualified to assume the responsibility for a child's well-being.

A Vitality-Enhancing Lifestyle

Raising children requires stamina. Unless potential parents are committed to a healthy lifestyle, they will become exhausted from the demands of parenting. People who have trouble maintaining a healthy diet, a balanced daily routine of waking and sleeping, and regular exercise – and those who are struggling with addictive behaviors – will be limited in their ability to provide for a child's physical and emotional needs, as well as unable to serve as a healthy mirror for a developing child.

Skillful Communication

People who are unable to skillfully communicate their needs have reduced chances of getting them met. Most people learned to communicate their emotions by observing their parents, who learned from *their* parents. If we trace the pattern back to the original family of Adam and Eve, and acknowledge how their children turned out, we must accept that human beings are not innately great communicators! Fortunately, communication skills can be improved with education and practice.

Balanced Boundary Management

Successful living requires having healthy boundaries. Young children cannot be expected to set their own, so establishing the right balance between protection and nourishment is among the most important responsibilities of loving parents. Inappropriate boundary violations through emotional, physical, or sexual abuse can have lifelong harmful consequences.

Parents who are excessively rigid about boundary setting can also thwart healthy emotional development, even if inadvertently. Instilling extreme fears about a dangerous world suppresses a child's natural curiosity and enthusiasm about self-expansion. A balanced approach requires parenting finesse.

Too Little, Too Much

I recently worked with two women who illustrate the effects of poor boundary management. Paige, the fifth of six children, remembers receiving very little guidance from her overwhelmed parents. Her all-night forays as a young teenager were scarcely noticed, and despite her escalating acting-out through casual sex, frequent drug experimentation, and barely passing grades, the only attention she received from her parents was a few minimally enforced groundings. Her lack of self-esteem stemmed from her internalized belief, *No one cared enough about me to say no.*

The second woman, Joanne, was an only child born to parents who married later in life. Her mother, a successful professional, did not conceive until her early forties. Throughout her upbringing, Joanne scarcely remembers a time when she was encouraged to make her own choices. Her mom exercised control over her clothing, hairstyle, and extracurricular activities. Over Joanne's vigorous objections, her mother sent her away to the same boarding school she had attended as a girl. Joanne's explanation for her lack of self-confidence was, *I never had the opportunity to make my own mistakes.*

Re-Parenting

Boundary setting can be learned, but it requires awareness and practice. Once established, healthy boundaries protect us from harm while allowing nourishing experiences to enter and expand us. If your caregivers, like so many, were deficient in these core skills, you will most likely need some emotional healing work. Over the years, many popular approaches have focused on helping us re-parent our inner child. It is my experience that healing our *inner parents* is just as important, if we are to release the old emotional residue that is binding our heart and become free to love and free to heal.

Step to Freedom

Consider the skill set of your parents or caregivers as you were growing up. Review the five core traits (self-awareness, emotional availability, a vitality-enhancing lifestyle, skillful communication, balanced boundary management) and rate your mother and father on each, using a scale of 0 (very poor) to 5 (excellent). Then rate yourself on these same qualities, honestly identifying where you see a need for improvement.

Taking Inventory

The fruit of emotional healing is happiness. When embarking on any journey, it is important to recognize where you are now and where you want to go, so that you can map out the best route for getting there. The inventory below is designed to help you assess your current state. As you engage in the work of releasing that which does not serve you and opening to that which does, your score – and your sense of well-being – will improve.

Please answer the following questions to identify your emotional state at this point in your life. Use the scale below.

0 = almost never

1 = rarely

2 = occasionally

3 = frequently

4 = much of the time

5 = almost always

1.	Regardless of what is happening around me, I know I am a lovable person.	
2.	Even when facing significant challenges, I trust I will weather the storm and be okay.	
3.	I care for myself through healthy choices that reflect my intrinsic self-worth.	
4.	I am comfortable spending time alone without feeling lonely.	
5.	I am able to set healthy boundaries with the people in my life.	
6.	I have peaceful relationships with my parents, siblings, and family members.	

7. I trust my intuitive inner voice, even when others attempt to discourage me.	
8. I am comfortable with my body image.	
9. I can handle rejection without questioning my core worthiness.	
10. I recognize and acknowledge my unique talents and am at ease in expressing them.	
11. Although at times I may experience episodes of anxiety or sadness, I know that these are passing moods that will resolve.	
12. I am authentic in my most intimate relationships; I am not leading a "double life."	
13. I can effectively communicate my needs to those in my life.	
14. I am passionate and enthusiastic about what I am doing.	
15. I do not harbor disappointments, grievances, or regrets.	
16. I am in tune with, and accepting of, my biological appetites and needs.	
17. I am comfortable giving and receiving affection.	
18. I enjoy my sexuality without limiting inhibitions.	
19. I respond to feedback with an openness to improve and without accepting another's perspective as unquestionably accurate.	
20. I am inherently trusting and trustworthy in my relationships.	
Total Points	

With a maximum possible total of 100 points, a score above 85 suggests that you have a healthy self-image and are not substantially encumbered with unprocessed emotional residue from your past. If you've been honest with your answers, you have a high sense of self-worth, do a good job of managing your boundaries, and take excellent care of yourself. For the most part, your relationships are peaceful and nurturing, and you can effortlessly experience pleasure.

A score between 65 and 85 usually implies that you have a "normal" level of emotional well-being. You are "fine." You may sense the possibility of feeling more alive than you do now, but may not be highly motivated to make any major changes in your life at this point. However, chances are good that as time passes, your ability and willingness to tolerate being "fine" will diminish, and the need or desire for more will emerge. If you fall into this category, I encourage you to mine this book for nuggets of gold that can enrich your life right now, holding an intention to make improvements that will enhance your emotional and physical well-being.

A score below 65 suggests that you did not receive consistently healthy messages about your intrinsic value as you were growing up. You are currently carrying an emotional burden of misunderstanding about who you are and what you deserve – you are in doubt or even denial of your inherent lovability. You are probably struggling with issues that continue to hurt your relationships with yourself and others. Life is too short and too miraculous an opportunity for love for you to keep carrying this load. I encourage you to take the steps outlined in this book to liberate yourself from your past misunderstandings and disappointments . . . to set yourself emotionally free.

Restoring the Foundation of Well-Being

I've never met anyone with a perfect upbringing. It seems to me that life on planet Earth just doesn't work that way. The basic challenges of getting our needs met and managing boundaries are inherent in growing up human. All of us have struggled to some degree. Those who have experienced a greater share of complexities and complications are likely to carry more substantial misunderstandings in their mind and distress in their body. The residue of incompletely processed emotional wounds from the past leads to emotional constrictions and the depletion of vitality.

No matter what has happened up until this point, you have the right and the capacity to be happy. By working through the process provided in this book, you will identify where you are holding emotional toxicity, take steps to release it, reestablish the healthy flow of life energy, and finally release yourself from the pain of the past. These are the steps to healing. This is the path to freedom.

In this chapter you have already taken the first step towards the heart of healing simply by exploring how your earliest experiences shaped your core beliefs about yourself, and by taking an inventory of your emotional state. In the next chapter, we will go deeper into the healing process as you identify the stories you have been telling yourself about who you are, what you deserve, and what has brought you to this point in your life. You will begin to loosen the hold these stories have on you as you discover the core misunderstandings at the heart of them – and realize that you are and have always been lovable.

Chapter Two

Core Misunderstandings: Identifying Your Stories

The heart is right to cry,
When even the smallest drop of light, of love
Is taken away.

— HAFIZ

As YOU BEGIN TO IDENTIFY THE EARLY STORIES AND MISUNDERSTANDINGS that have contributed to the emotional pain in your life, I want to introduce a few powerful concepts from Ayurveda, the ancient healing system of India. Ayurveda offers a valuable approach to emotional and physical health – a holistic perspective that recognizes that the two are, in fact, inseparable. The Ayurvedic physicians of 5,000 years ago knew something that has now been verified by modern science: the mind, including our thoughts, emotions, and desires, is inextricably connected to our body. At the deepest level, they are one indistinguishable unit – a river of intelligence shaped by our choices, experiences, reactions, and beliefs.

Ayurveda teaches that physical and emotional health depends upon our body's ability to metabolize all aspects of life. This includes not only the food we eat, but also our experiences, emotions, and sensory impressions. The metabolic power responsible for extracting nourishment and releasing toxicity is known as *agni* – a Sanskrit word meaning "fire." Linguistically, agni is the etymological root of the English words *ignition* and *ignite,* and we can think of agni as our digestive fire.

When our agni is robust, we are able to digest food efficiently and easily assimilate our daily experiences. We absorb what is nourishing and let go of that which doesn't serve, enabling us to make healthy blood cells, muscle tissue, bones, and nerves. Just as a roaring blaze in a fireplace creates warmth and heat, burning even a damp log down to fine ash, a strong agni produces vitality and enthusiasm, completely "cooking" the experiences of our lives. When our agni is weak, however, we can't extract value or benefit from our experiences, even those that are potentially nourishing. A weak fire generates an excessive amount of smoke, leaving behind charred pieces of wood that – to continue the analogy – are similar to the toxic residue that remains when our digestive power is poor. This accumulated residue weakens our health and blocks the flow of energy and information throughout our body, making us feel dull and listless.

The Undigested Past

Ayurveda teaches that the underlying cause of all disease is the build-up of toxins, or *ama* as it is called in Sanskrit. From this perspective, dietary saturated fat is toxic if you consume more than your body is capable of metabolizing. Over time, this leads to blockage of blood vessels and arteries and, ultimately, to heart attacks. Atherosclerosis is a physical example of how undigested residues of past experience can interfere with the free flow of energy in the present.

While it's easy to understand agni and ama in terms of food, it's important to remember that your mind and heart are continually digesting energy and information as well. Your mental digestive powers are working right now to break down the ideas you are reading into components your intellect can assimilate. Similarly, your emotional agni processes your experiences and feelings, including the beautiful smile of a loved one, unexpected criticism at work, or the excitement of a new relationship.

If your emotional agni is strong, you are able to extract whatever is nourishing from your experiences and interactions with people and eliminate the rest. The inability to metabolize emotions, on the other hand, can produce as much or more ama or toxic residue as undigested food. In fact, pent-up anger, long-held sadness, and lingering guilt are for many people more debilitating to their psychological and physical health than any problem with their physical digestion.

Painful psychological experiences that exceed our capacity for digestion can result in emotional ama that disrupts our ability to be fully available in our present relationships. Experiences of abuse or neglect accumulate in our emotional heart, limiting the flow of love in and out. The toxic residue of incompletely digested mistreatment, disappointment, resentment, or regret inhibits our ability to give and receive love.

Purification to Rejuvenation

One of the cornerstones of Ayurvedic medicine is a powerful five-step detoxification therapy in which a series of massage and cleansing treatments are used to release the physical and emotional toxins stored in the body. The steps of this purification process are:

1) Preparation and Facilitation
2) Identification
3) Mobilization
4) Release
5) Rejuvenation

The Free to Love process that I will guide you through in the following chapters mirrors the five steps of this ancient Ayurvedic therapy. While you won't be following a simplified diet, taking detoxifying herbs, or receiving Ayurvedic body treatments (though I highly recommend getting massages to support your emotional clearing), reading this book and completing the exercises are components of a powerful process to release toxicity from your heart and mind, clearing the channels for radiant well-being.

In the next chapter, you will be introduced to a program of yoga postures, breathing exercises, and meditation techniques designed to facilitate the identification, mobilization, and release of emotional ama. Let's now start the detoxification process by identifying the early stories and core misunderstandings that contribute to emotional ama.

Variations on the Original Script

The trajectory of our life is established before we are capable of consciously questioning what it is we're aiming for. Under the direction of parents, caregivers, teachers, and clergy – and through the feedback of siblings and peers – we're informed of who we are, what qualities are valued, those beliefs we should hold to be true, the talents we possess (and lack), and the goals that are worth pursuing.

If your parents were loving, attentive, and flexible, they helped you discover your authentic identity and purpose in life without rigidly imposing their expectations on you. If they were overwhelmed, distracted, or unyielding, you may have been subjected to a constant barrage of "shoulds" and "should nots" as your inner nature struggled with their controlling nurture. This constant friction can erode self-esteem as you attempt to become the person you are expected to be. Children are deeply influenced by the conversations taking place around them and internalize the information as if it were true.

People are both alike and different. We all pass through core physical and psychological stages. We all learn to navigate the environment of our homes, schools, religious institutions, and communities in the process of developing a personality. Each of us has singular struggles and experiences woven into the fabric of our individuality.

While acknowledging the uniqueness of the tales people share with me, I have discovered that a few common themes regularly emerge. After many years of listening to patients carrying emotional ama, I've identified six core storylines:

1) The absent parent
2) The impaired parent
3) The sick parent
4) The distracted parent
5) The controlling parent
6) The abusive parent/relative/family friend

These stories are never comfortable to hear, but bringing them into the open is the first step in the healing process. Lifelong emotional struggles often derive from one of these early stories, which set the trajectories for our lives. It is likely that one or more of these stories will resonate to some degree with your own life history. I hope that in reading them, you will see that your personal tale is part of the universal human story – that you will realize that *you are not the only one*. I also hope that it will inspire you to free yourself from the limitations of your painful past and begin writing a more fulfilling next chapter in your life. Always remember, you deserve to heal your emotional wounds and to be happy.

The Story of the Absent Parent

John's parents met in college and quickly fell into a passionate relationship. Within two months, John's mother became pregnant. They discussed abortion but decided that fate meant for them to be together. They married when she was five months pregnant, but within a few months, John's father was feeling intensely claustrophobic and started staying out late with his friends. He was present for the delivery but moved out when John was two months old.

John saw his father a few times in his early childhood, but lost contact once he became a teenager. He remembers his mom being perpetually overwhelmed, and he continues to believe that he is a burden on the people he loves. He struggles with a number of health problems, including recurrent episodes of asthma. His breathing problems are not helped by his obesity, which he attributes to using food to alleviate his anxiety.

This story of abandonment is all too common. Nature has made it easy to conceive a child in just a few moments, but even the most intense intimate encounter may be inadequate to forge a commitment between sexual partners. We sometimes hear of mothers abandoning their children, but more often than not, it is the man who is unable to accept parenting responsibilities.

Child rearing is demanding and unrelenting work. Committed couples struggle with allocating time and resources between their own relationship, child-rearing responsibilities, and basic life needs. The challenges facing single parents may be exponentially more demanding as they bear the sole responsibility of providing financial and emotional support.

If this theme resonates with your story, your healing requires that you relinquish personal responsibility for your parent's abandonment. Your absent mother or father did not leave because of you; they left as a result of their inability to assume responsibility beyond their own immediate needs. The emotional and physical exhaustion of the remaining parent or caregiver was likewise not your fault. Babies and children are not capable of meeting their own needs, and therefore are dependent upon their caregivers, who must prioritize their children's requirements above their own. The fact that your parents were psychologically ill-equipped to meet your needs is not evidence of your deficiency. The bottom line is: *It's not your fault.*

As we move through this process, I will encourage you to identify and tell your story, move through the feelings associated with it, and release the mistaken core beliefs about your self-worth that you derived from it. Then you will be ready to understand, forgive, and move forward with a more open heart, enabling you to create more happiness, better health, and the nourishing relationships you deserve.

The Story of the Impaired Parent

Susan's father was an alcoholic with an unpredictable disposition, alternating between anger and withdrawal. Although he never physically hurt Susan's mother, Susan witnessed her parents physically scuffling on several occasions. The arguments she overheard after going to bed were particularly distressing to Susan. To avoid conflict, she learned to be as invisible as possible whenever her dad was at home.

As an adult, Susan did not discover that her husband had a drinking problem until a couple of years into their marriage. When he began verbally abusing her, she threatened to leave him, but he promised to change. Despite little evidence that he will ever follow through on his commitment, she has been unable to extricate herself from the relationship.

In addition to chronic insomnia, Susan has recurrent migraine headaches. Under the care of numerous neurologists, she has been prescribed more than a dozen medications in as many years, with only limited results and generally intolerable side effects.

Alcoholism hurts both alcoholics and those close to them. Children raised by one or two alcoholic parents suffer a type of post-traumatic stress disorder. Long after they have grown up and moved away from home, people who were raised around alcohol or other addictions often struggle with ongoing emotional and physical challenges.

The unpredictable moods of an alcoholic parent can destabilize a child's emotional set point. If a parent has also inflicted emotional or physical abuse, their children may have difficulty trusting in relationships as adults. In addition, it's very common for the children of alcoholics to develop alcohol or drug abuse problems themselves as they grow up. At a subconscious level, they have learned from their parents how to anesthetize painful feelings with an addiction, even if the method is only marginally effective.

Other obsessive addictions can have similarly toxic effects. A mother or father addicted to drugs, gambling, the internet, or work will be less emotionally available. Children interpret this lack of attention as a message that their needs are a low priority and that who they are isn't very important either. Without the support of loving, nurturing parents, they are likely to develop low self-worth and little self-confidence.

Escaping from this prison of toxic conditioning requires dedicated attention to identifying the patterns, relinquishing guilt about being unable to fix the impaired parent, and developing a new, positive inner dialogue that honors one's unconditional value. If the theme of the impaired parent is part of your own story, it will also be essential to work through and release the inevitable anger you've been carrying. Before you can truly forgive and be free to love, you will need to give yourself permission to fully experience, then release, the anger you have pushed down for so many years.

The Story of the Sick Parent

When Belinda was five years old, her mother developed severe joint pain. After months of diagnostic studies, she was diagnosed with a rare arthritic disorder that could be managed but not cured. For weeks at a time, Belinda's mother was incapacitated by pain, at times unable to leave her bed. Her husband's modest income wasn't enough to pay for the help they needed, so Belinda increasingly found herself assuming household responsibilities, including caring for her younger sister.

Belinda's bouts of depression started as a teenager and became progressively more debilitating in her twenties. Although she was able to function on antidepressant medications, she experienced little enthusiasm or joy. She describes herself as being obsessed with perfection and says that she feels intense anxiety whenever she senses she is losing control.

One of the most difficult awakenings for children is when they recognize that their parents are neither all-powerful nor all-knowing. In my own life, this turning point happened at the age of eleven, during the Cuban missile crisis of 1962, when I realized that my parents could not solve a problem that threatened to destroy our world.

Children feel secure when they assume adults are in control and capable of protecting them. When a parent becomes sick or disabled from a physical or psychological ailment, it forces children to prematurely forsake their innocence and confront the reality that the world is not always a safe place.

When a parent is chronically ill or disabled, the same-sex child often begins to assume that parent's role, without the requisite emotional or physical maturity. A little girl may begin to act like Mother; a little boy may try to become the man of the house. Birth order also tends to play a role, with the oldest child more likely to take on responsibilities for the whole family.

When childhood innocence is curtailed, unresolved issues may show up in adulthood. People who have grown up with a sick parent commonly suffer from depression and anxiety. Their capacity for lightheartedness and joy is often limited because when they were children, the adults around them may have explicitly disparaged expressions of happiness as frivolous, given the gravity of the parent's illness. Although resentment and anger may lurk below the surface, they may consciously express the view that "indulging" or addressing these emotions is an unaffordable luxury. Mirroring the illness of the sick parent is not unusual.

For those who have experienced some variation of this core story, healing and becoming emotionally free require identifying the underlying disappointment and giving oneself permission to engage in activities that generate happiness, even if they aren't "goal-focused" or "productive." Those willing to heal learn that "taking care of business" has limited value if it is not accompanied by love and joy.

The Story of the Distracted Parent

The first child of adoring parents, Amanda remembers her earliest years as safe and loving. Her younger brother, born when Amanda turned three, was challenging almost from the day he was brought home. He had difficulty establishing a rhythm and was frequently inconsolable when he cried. When he failed to meet his speech and motor developmental milestones, a series of investigations led to the diagnosis of autism.

The demands of her brother exhausted Amanda's parents, who had limited emotional resources left over for Amanda. She couldn't help but resent him even though she knew that he had no control over his condition.

As an adult, she married an ambitious entrepreneur who was driven to build personal wealth and was often away on business trips. Despite receiving reassurances of his love and commitment, Amanda felt insecure and alone.

Four years into the marriage, Amanda began feeling tired, even upon first awakening in the morning. Her malaise increased dramatically after only modest exercise. She began having episodes of swollen glands in her neck and vague, flu-like symptoms. After a series of medical evaluations spanning a year, she was diagnosed with chronic fatigue syndrome.

Life is complex and presents situations that are beyond our direct control. When as children we face life challenges that we have no power to change, it is difficult not to internalize the chaos, conflict, or uncertainty. Children do not have a well-developed internal reference against which they can compare deviations, for they only know what they have experienced in their own lives. The chaotic, disordered state becomes their "normal," but never feels completely comfortable.

Since their sense of self and self-worth are still developing, children whose parents are distracted may internalize the belief that they don't deserve undivided loving attention. Adults can compensate for the "attention deficit" they experienced as children by becoming conscious of the power of attention and consciously requesting it in their relationships. It may simply mean asking the important people in your life to look at you when you are speaking to them, or asking them to complete whatever else they are doing first, rather than offering you their partial attention. No one should be satisfied with crumbs of attention. As we will explore in coming chapters, *attention* and *intention* are the two most powerful tools we can use to increase our success and happiness in life.

Insufficiency to Abundance

The stories up to this point have been variations on the theme of unavailability. As a result of our parents' emotional overwhelm, illness, impairment, or distraction, we may not have received the adoring feedback we needed and deserved to form a healthy, valued sense of self. To experience the freedom to love, you will need to release the inner messages of insufficiency and inadequacy that arise from having an unavailable parent, and replace them with messages of authentic self-worth and abundance. You can realize this transformation by connecting with a deeper domain within you – the core of your being – and by cultivating relationships that are based upon equality and respect. In the pages that follow, you will learn practical tools for fulfilling both of these aims.

Crossing the Line

The final two themes tell the story of emotional or physical boundary encroachments. The primary task of healthy parents is to help their offspring establish healthy boundaries that allow nourishing energy and information to come in, while keeping harmful input out. This can apply to food (healthy allowed in; junk kept out), air (fresh allowed in; smoke kept out), friends (nice allowed in; nasty kept out), and beliefs (tolerance allowed in; bigotry kept out).

When adults have not learned to manage their own boundaries, they tend to violate those who are vulnerable, and often this means children. There are various levels of intrusion – from excessive psychological control to emotional, physical, and sexual abuse. The more serious the violation, the more difficult it is for an individual to maintain healthy boundaries as an adult.

The Story of the Intrusive Parent

Emily's mother, a child of the Sixties, had few external boundaries while growing up. Emily remembers hearing stories about her mother, who as a young child was left free to wander around at her parents' parties, where guests were drinking alcohol, smoking pot, and engaging in nearly public displays of sex.

Years later, when Emily's mom was pregnant, she was determined not to repeat the pattern. As a result, Emily had the strictest upbringing of any of her friends. No aspect of her life was free from her mother's direct influence or control. By the time Emily reached adolescence, her days were as regimented as a boot camp recruit or a convent novitiate. Her mother had no qualms about listening in on her phone conversations, rummaging through her drawers, and imposing severe disciplinary actions for the slightest infractions.

As soon as she turned eighteen, Emily revolted, leaving her home and wasting little time in making up for what she perceived as years of deprivation. Having received little opportunity to establish her own boundaries, she spent the next several years testing her limits with risky behaviors. When at the age of twenty-two she had an epileptic seizure triggered by escalating cocaine use, she decided it was time to ask herself who she wanted to be when she grew up.

Although some talk show psychologists may suggest that good parents can never be too controlling over their children's choices, I believe that balance is the key to health in all aspects of life. If a parent, in reaction to their own sense of inadequate boundaries, becomes overly authoritarian, children may fail to learn self-discipline and the ability to take responsibility for their own choices. When parents use fear and punishment as their primary tools for enforcing good behavior, resentment festers and ultimately erupts. Long after they are on their own, people who grew up with a dictatorial or tyrannical parent may continue the rebellious or resistive inner dialogue, which may translate into self-destructive choices.

People in this situation often find themselves having an ongoing argument with the controlling parent who has taken up residence within their mind. If you realize that as you are arguing with an inner parent, you are engaging in behaviors that do not serve you, you will need to learn how to separate the information about what is better or worse for you from the emotional charge. Behaviors that assert your independence but fail to enhance your self-worth will prove to be expensive life lessons. There are better ways to spend your precious life energy.

The Story of the Sexually Abusive Parent (or other relative or adult)

Camille's biological father died in an auto accident when she was three years old. When Camille was eleven, her mother married a man who was several years her senior and had a seventeen-year-old son. Initially, Camille appreciated her stepbrother's attention, but she felt confused when he started climbing into bed with her after the adults were asleep. She was conflicted about wanting his attention but uncomfortable with the way he touched her. Once she began to develop sexually, his actions became more aggressive. When his invasive touching caused her discomfort, she finally insisted that he stop.

Over the next two years she gained an inordinate amount of weight and has struggled with overeating ever since. To this day, she cannot explain why she never told her mother what happened.

Childhood sexual abuse is a serious problem. Since most cases go unreported, estimates are imprecise, but according to many studies more than 25 percent of women, and more than 15 percent of men, have been victims of childhood sexual abuse. In addition to the direct emotional and physical pain, these boundary violations contribute to long-term psychological and physical distress.

A recent study of women with chronic headaches found that more than one-third had suffered physical or sexual abuse as a child. Childhood abuse has been associated with increased risks for anxiety, depression, substance abuse, obesity, eating disorders, irritable bowel syndrome, and fibromyalgia. As brought to light by the recent acknowledgment of clergy sexual abuse in the Catholic Church, these violations profoundly affect how people think and feel about themselves, others, and their relationship to the world.

People who suffered childhood sexual abuse often compound their injury with the insult of guilt. If you were abused as a child, you must recognize that *it was not your fault*. Although as an adult you may be able to consider how you could have responded differently, as a child you had limited emotional and mental resources. It is not a child's responsibility to set boundaries, particularly with an older relative or family friend.

It is not surprising that, like Camille, people who were sexually abused as children often develop eating disorders and other issues with food. There are many possible explanations for why this might occur. Some victims of sexual abuse may gain weight or become excessively thin or anorexic out of a subconscious belief that becoming less physically attractive will deter the abuser. In addition, the pleasurable sensations of eating or the sense of control gained from rigidly restricting food intake may temporarily reduce anxiety. At times, an eating issue is a form of self-punishment, reflecting the guilt a person is carrying. In all of these cases, identifying the story is the first step to healing.

The path to becoming free to love and thus free to heal requires guidance. Sharing your story with a counselor who can empathize and bring clarity to your experience can be helpful. Identifying and giving a voice to the complex feelings that arise and engaging in rituals of release will open the channels for emotional toxicity to leave and nourishment to enter. There is a time for forgiveness, but not before you have named, expressed, and released the emotional pain created by boundary violations. We will be exploring these steps in the next few chapters.

Step to Freedom

Write your original script. Take time to reflect upon the circumstances of your conception, incubation, birth, and childhood. If you recognize that there are substantial gaps in your memory of your early story, ask the people who were there – your mother, father, siblings, other relatives, and close family friends – to help you fill in the details. This information and knowledge will set you on the path to healing.

Time for a New Story

As we have seen, our early stories drive us to make choices that reinforce our early patterns. They place us on a path that many of us keep following for the rest of our lives. If you are in emotional pain or have been struggling with a chronic health problem you suspect has an emotional component, now is the time to find a happier road to travel by revealing the unconscious script that has been directing your life. If your early experiences failed to support you in the formation of a healthy self-image that allows you to know at the deepest level of your being that you are worthy, valuable, and lovable, it is time to recognize and relinquish your core conditioned misunderstandings. It is time to begin writing a new script that accurately reflects the beautiful, powerful, and worthy being you are.

*

Having read this far in the book, you now have a deeper understanding of how we develop our core beliefs about ourselves and why it is so crucial to release the emotional residue of the past – the ama – that has prevented us from experiencing the pure love and joy at the heart of our being. In the next chapter, we will engage your body and breath in preparation for identifying the specific emotional ama you are carrying.

Chapter Three

Preparing for Freedom

If you cried in heaven, everyone would laugh
For they would know you were just kidding.
— SAINT CATHERINE OF SIENA

PREPARING TO LET GO BEGINS WITH INTENTION. A CORE PRINCIPLE IN both Ayurveda and yoga is that our intentions have organizing power. The more clearly you can envision what you want to create in your life, the more powerfully you can align your body, mind, heart, and soul to achieve the outcome you are seeking. Hopefully, by this point you have the unequivocal intention to clear the path to emotional freedom so that your heart can open to giving and receiving love. This chapter will help you focus your intention, set your desired trajectory, and awaken the vital energy of your body to empower your quest for healing and freedom.

Through my experience of helping people work through emotional pain, I've learned that the heart is the portal between the mind and body. Instead of relying solely on your intellect, you need to invite your heart and body to be part of the process. A purely mental or analytic approach usually isn't enough. Although your mind may try to think its way into emotional freedom, your good intentions will lose their momentum without the full support of your body. The body, upon receiving the invitation to participate, can be a powerful ally in healing the emotional wounds that constrict the heart.

Every experience in the mind is accompanied by shifts in the chemistry and electricity of the body. Whenever you say, "I feel anxious, angry, disappointed, or hopeless," you are acknowledging that your body is generating disturbing sensations. These sensations result from shifts in hormone levels and in the pattern of nerve firings within your nervous system. These physiological shifts can persist well beyond emotionally upsetting experiences. Over time, your physiology reflects your emotional history and reinforces your expectations about the future.

Just as changing patterns of thought can influence the body, changing the position of the body can influence the mind and facilitate emotional release. Stretching your muscles and expanding your range of motion shift the bodily patterns that trap emotional pain. The yoga poses, breathing techniques, and meditation practices presented here are designed to subtly yet profoundly prepare your mind to begin the releasing process.

Heart-Opening Yoga

The ancient wisdom tradition of yoga offers practices that prepare the mind and heart to release what is not useful and to open to that which is. Since body, breath, and mind are intimately connected, practices that enliven one dimension influence the others. Therefore, we want to begin with a set of heart-opening movements, known as *asanas*.

Asana is a Sanskrit word that means "seat." What is typically known as yoga today in the Western world is a system of postures that enhance the body's flexibility, balance, and strength. The primary purpose of these poses is to create such ease in the body that the mind is able to expand. If you are carrying tension in your neck, pain in your shoulders, or stiffness in your lower back, it will be difficult for your mind to go beyond thoughts of discomfort when you close your eyes and look within. Therefore, taking time to open your body in preparation for opening your heart is worthwhile.

I encourage you to practice these seven heart-opening poses at a level of intensity that reflects your self-nurturing intention. Forcing or straining while performing your stretches usually inhibits rather than fosters release. Enter into each pose with your full awareness, moving to the point of resistance, not pain. With your eyes closed, allow yourself to feel the tension in your muscles with each posture, but do not go beyond this point into discomfort. Breathing consciously, soften your body with each outflow of your breath, surrendering into the resistance rather than forcing your way through it.

Perform these seven poses in sequence, with the intention for your body to open in preparation for deep emotional release. Move through each posture with appreciation and respect for your body. Honoring the wisdom of your body by listening to its signals of comfort and discomfort enrolls its support in accessing, mobilizing, and releasing toxic emotions. If you have a known injury or physical limitation, perform these postures with great sensitivity. If you have any doubt about whether you can do a pose comfortably, **skip it.**

1) Sky to Earth Pose

It is best to perform this pose in a standing position, but you may choose to do it from a seated position if necessary.

Begin by bringing your palms and fingers together in "prayer" position, feeling your thumbs gently touching the area of your heart. Close your eyes and take several slow, deep breaths.

Very gradually, begin moving both hands upwards. When they reach about forehead level, interlace your fingers while continuing to raise your hands over your head. When your arms are fully extended, rotate your wrists outward while your fingers remain entwined.

While slowly exhaling, begin flexing your body as you fold forward, bringing your arms down and relaxing your neck. Gradually collapse through your upper, middle, and lower back, walking your hands down your thighs, moving your outstretched hands towards your feet. It is not important whether or not you can touch your feet.

Continue extending with your arms, shoulders, and spine, arching up and backwards, feeling the stretch in your chest and abdomen. Look up at your interlaced fingers. If you feel you can maintain your balance, rise up onto your toes to complete the full extension.

When you have flexed forward as far as you can, close your eyes and relax into this position, slowly inhaling and exhaling for several breaths. With each outflow of your breath, soften through your neck, back, shoulders, and hips.

As you inhale, gently raise yourself upright, again lifting both arms over your head, stretching as far upwards as you comfortably can.

Again, rise up onto your toes if you feel you can maintain your balance.

Complete the pose by slowly returning
your hands to the level of your heart.

2) Swaying Palm Pose

Begin this second posture in the same manner as the *Sky to Earth* pose, with both of your hands together at the level of your heart. Again stretch upwards until you are fully extended.

Slowly begin to arch your body to the left, stretching through your arms, shoulder, side, and hip. Hold the arch, breathing into the stretch with slow, deep breaths, lengthening with each exhalation.

Slowly return to an upright position, and then gradually arch your body to the right, stretching through your left shoulder, side, and hip. Inhale and exhale, gently lengthening your stretch with each outflow of your breath.

Slowly return to an upright position and then gently lower your arms.

3) Pelvis-Opening Pose

This next pose enlivens awareness in the body's second energy center or *chakra*. This site is classically associated with primitive emotions, sexuality, and creativity. Because of the powerful messages many young girls often receive about "keeping their legs together," this pose can sometimes awaken strong feelings and images. Perform it in a safe setting where you can explore the emotions and information that emerge.

Lying on your back, place both hands over your heart. Bring your knees up so the soles of your feet are on the floor.

Now slowly lower your knees toward the floor, opening at your hips. Open to the point where you feel tension, then gently pull your ankles towards your groin. Breathe deeply into your pelvic region while maintaining your awareness in your hips. Without straining, relax and release with each exhalation.

Repeat this process several times, gently releasing further with each opening. Then, slowly extend your knees and rest on your back.

4) Pelvic Lift Pose

Lying on your back, bend your knees
and plant your feet on the floor.
Reach with outstretched arms towards your feet, holding your ankles
with your hands. If you cannot reach
your ankles, place your palms on
the floor with your fingers pointing
towards your heels.

Keeping the back of your head on the floor, lift your pelvis up in the air, stretching through your chest and abdomen. Take several slow, deep breaths in and out through your nose.

Slowly lower your bottom to the floor and then repeat the movement, lifting up your hips while stretching through your midsection. After several more slow deep breaths, lower yourself to the floor and extend your legs.

5) Cobra Pose

Lying on your stomach, place your
hands on the floor under your shoulders. Predominantly using your back
muscles, lift your chest off the floor.
Use your hands to provide support
while you inhale.

Stretch and extend through your neck, even raising your eyes upwards as if trying to see the top of your head. Take several slow, deep breaths, then gradually lower your chest to the floor. Repeat this pose several times.

6) Open Twist Pose

Lying on your back, stretch out both arms to your sides at right angles to your body.

Bend your left knee and bring your left foot over your right leg, placing it on the floor next to your right knee. While your lower spine and pelvis are twisting to the right, turn your head and neck to the left, feeling the stretch through your spine. Take several slow breaths, releasing further into the pose with each exhalation.

Return to midline, with both legs on the floor.

Then, bending your right knee, place your right foot across your left leg next to your left knee. While rotating your lower body to the left, turn your head to the right, again feeling the stretch throughout the spine while taking slow, deep breaths. Return to resting position with both legs extended on the floor.

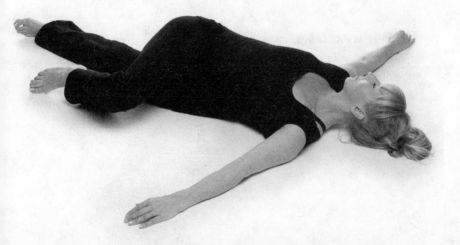

7) Child's Pose

This final pose promotes safety and centering in preparation for inner exploration.

Beginning on your belly, bring your knees up with your legs and ankles together. Leaning forward, slowly flex at the waist until your chest is resting on your thighs and your forehead is on the floor.

Stretch your arms over your head in front of you and take several slow, deep breaths.

Then bring your arms back towards your ankles until they are resting alongside your legs. Feel the movement of your chest on your knees as you slowly inhale and exhale with awareness. Remain in this position for several minutes, noticing your thoughts and sensations.

Heart-Opening Breathing Exercises

The next step in preparing to clear the heart of negative emotional residue is to become intimate with the purifying power of your breath. From time immemorial in cultures around the world, people have used breath work to change their awareness and shift perspective. From the ancient pranayama yogic breathing techniques of India to Stanislav Grof's Holotropic Breathwork, conscious breathing adds transformational power to healing intentions.

Breathing provides a doorway between our conscious and unconscious patterns of thought and behavior. Deep primitive centers in the brain regulate the rate, rhythm, and depth of respiration, dynamically adapting to our changing perceptions and interpretations of the world. Whenever we feel threatened, our mind and body become activated to either flee from or aggressively attack the perceived danger. Spontaneously, our breathing adjusts to our interpretations, influencing and responding to shifts in our neurological, hormonal, and circulatory systems.

Most of the time, the intimate connection between our breath, mind, and body is automatic. We don't have to pay attention to our breath for it to operate. It's as if the universe is performing cosmic CPR on us day and night.

Unlike many other automatic functions of our body, however, our breath can be consciously controlled. We learn this as small children when we hold our breath to get a response from our siblings or parents. You may have experimented with hyperventilation, noticing how you can make yourself dizzy. Just as activity in the mind and body influences the breath, the reverse is also true – altering the breath influences the mind and body.

Clearing the Passages

Breath work can be relaxing and invigorating, serving to clear the mind and open the heart. Try these three techniques and notice the thoughts in your mind and the sensations in your body. If you are currently pregnant, have been diagnosed with a seizure disorder, or have a known heart or lung condition, perform these breathing exercises very gently. If you feel any discomfort while you are doing this breath work, listen to your body and **stop.**

1) Bellows Breath

Sitting comfortably with your eyes closed, place your hands on your thighs. Using your diaphragm and abdominal muscles, perform your inhalations and exhalations through your nose with a deep and rhythmic pace.

Begin breathing at the rate of about one breath every two seconds (30 breaths per minute.) After about one minute, slow and deepen your breath so that you are completing one cycle every four seconds (15 breaths per minute).

After another minute, slow your breathing down further, so that you are completing a full breath every ten to fifteen seconds (4 to 6 breaths per minute). Then allow your breathing to return to normal and simply observe your mind and body.

2) Radiant Breath

This next breathing technique uses a forceful exhalation through the nose, followed by a passive inhalation through the mouth.

Begin with your hands in a prayer position at your heart with your bent elbows pointing away from your sides. As you inhale through your mouth, rotate your elbows out and back, separating your palms and opening your chest.

As you forcefully exhale through your nose, bring your hands back together. Repeat this ten times at a rate of about one cycle per second. It may be helpful to have some facial tissue or a handkerchief available to clear your nostrils.

Wait about fifteen seconds and then repeat the process, inhaling through your mouth and exhaling through your nose, this time for fifteen breaths. After completing the cycle, rest with your eyes closed, observing your mind and body.

After another fifteen seconds, perform a third and final round, completing a cycle of twenty breaths in through your mouth and out through your nose, while expanding and contracting your chest through the rotating movement of your arms.

Take a few moments to simply observe the thoughts in your mind and sensations in your body.

3) Rhythmic Breath

This more intensive breathing technique is best performed with a partner at your side, but can be done on your own for shorter periods of time. It can be particularly powerful if you have emotionally moving classical music playing in the background. (See the notes in the Appendix for my suggestions.)

Begin lying on your side in a semi-fetal position. Place a pillow under your head and between your legs so that you are completely comfortable. Begin inhaling and exhaling deeply and rhythmically through your mouth at the rate of about one breath every two seconds.

As you continue at this pace, it is natural to experience mild mouth dryness and lightheadedness. If you begin to experience uncomfortable tingling, lightheadedness, or tightening of your muscles, reduce the depth and rate of your breathing. These physical symptoms occur when the blood becomes alkaline through hyperventilation, and the discomfort is a signal to slow down or stop this breathing practice.

Each time you practice rhythmic breathing, do it for about five minutes, noticing what is occurring in your mind and body. Pay particular attention to the information that emerges after you stop the breathing technique and allow your body to relax. It is common at this point for memories and strong emotions to surface.

Upon completion of these three breathing techniques, spend some time journaling about your experience. Write about your thoughts and feelings during and after each exercise, highlighting any insights that you may have gained.

Meditation: Glimpsing the Universal in the Personal

Our struggles in life derive from the dissonance that exists between our individualized needs and desires, and the unfolding of life as the universe sees fit. Reconciling our individuality with our universal essence is the real meaning of a spiritual quest. It's a great paradox that cannot be resolved at the level of the mind, but as the French philosopher Blaise Pascal observed, "The heart has reasons that reason cannot know." Through the wisdom of the heart, opposite values find their common ground beyond the discriminating nature of the mind. It is the nature of the heart, whenever it senses the possibility of unity, to ignore the arguments your mind may raise to justify conflict or opposition.

Heart-centered meditation can provide refuge from the turbulence of emotional commotion and a platform to access and work through emotional pain. Knowing that there is an inner sanctuary of harmony and wholeness that transcends the distress of loss, disappointment, betrayal, and violation enables us to face and vanquish the demons disturbing our peace.

There are as many meditation styles as there are modes of transportation. If a meditation technique takes you to a place of quiet inner reflection, it serves its role. For some, going on a walk can provide this valuable centering. For others, listening to classical music or guided visualizations can soothe a turbulent mind. Having taught meditation for more than three decades, I generally favor practices that require as little preparation or paraphernalia as possible. Although I've seen the value of recordings and biofeedback devices, I've learned that if you have as few excuses to not meditate as possible (e.g., forgot my CD player, ran out of batteries, headset not working, and so on), you will have the greatest possibility for gaining the benefits of a regular meditation practice.

Learning to Meditate

There are certain skills in life that are easy to learn, but require some instruction at the beginning. In my experience, meditation is one of these skills. Just as a responsible parent wouldn't give their child a video or book to learn how to swim or ride a bike, the optimal way to learn meditation is through hands-on instruction and guided practice. It's not that meditation is a difficult skill, but rather that early instruction can ensure competence that lasts a lifetime.

For this reason, we at the Chopra Center for Wellbeing developed a meditation certification program to create a worldwide network of instructors qualified to teach meditation in their communities. To access a certified *Primordial Sound Meditation* teacher in your area, please refer to the Appendix in the back of this book. Until you are able to receive formal instruction from a qualified teacher, practice the following breathing awareness meditation technique. It is easy to learn and will offer you many healing benefits on your path to emotional freedom.

"Quieting the Mind" Breathing Meditation

Sitting comfortably, close your eyes and take a few moments to scan your body. If you notice that you are holding any tension or strain in any muscle group, consciously relax that part of your body as you exhale deeply through your mouth.

Now simply observe the inflow and outflow of your breathing without trying to change it in any way. After observing your breath for about thirty seconds, silently begin repeating the word *I* on each inhalation and the word *am* on each exhalation. Repetition of *I am* should be gentle and vague, without concentration and without trying to clearly pronounce the words.

If you are performing the practice properly, there will be times when your awareness drifts away from your breath and the words *I am* as your mind entertains thoughts about the past or future. Whenever you notice that your attention has drifted away, gently return it to your breath and the words *I am*. Continue this process for fifteen to twenty minutes, then take a few minutes to stretch and move before resuming your usual activity.

Many people mistakenly think that they can't meditate because they have thoughts or distractions during their meditation. In fact, the only evidence that you are not meditating correctly is if you are straining. At least for these few minutes, relinquish your need to control the process and simply see what happens as you learn to let go. There are actually just four different experiences you can have during meditation, all of which are signs that you are doing it properly:

1) Awareness of your breathing and the words <u>I am</u>. Bringing your attention to this repetitive experience will help quiet your mental turbulence.

2) Trains of thought. At times your thoughts will seem to offer important insights; at other times, they will seem mundane. Often your thoughts will seem dreamlike and you won't be able to recall their actual content. Evaluating your thoughts isn't important. Instead, whenever you notice that you are thinking, simply return your attention to your breathing and the words *I am.*

3) *Sleep.* If you have not been getting enough rest lately, you may fall asleep while you are meditating. Don't resist the urge. If your system needs to rest, give it the opportunity to release accumulated fatigue. When you wake up, spend another five to ten minutes meditating.

4) *Clear mind.* There will be times when the thought traffic of your mind subsides and you have clarity of awareness without thinking. This is glimpsing the quiet space between your thoughts and is usually accompanied by a deep sense of physical relaxation. The experience of a clear mind in meditation begins to enliven a greater sense of witnessing awareness in your usual waking state. This awareness opens the possibility for more conscious choice-making. It enables you to move from a reflexive or reactive mode to a reflective mode of responding. From this platform of expanded perspective, you are in an empowered place to identify, mobilize, and release emotional toxicity.

Step to Freedom

Begin today to move your body. Put down this book and do at least three heart-opening poses. Perform one or more of the breathing techniques to energize you, and then spend at least a few minutes meditating and experiencing the quiet and peace within.

*

Emotional freedom is both the root and the fruit of a life lived in present moment awareness. This is only possible when all the dimensions of our life are unencumbered by the toxic residue of past experiences. Living in this state enables us to use our past but not allow our past to use us. You have already begun to open the communication channels between your body, breath, and mind, through heart-opening yoga postures, enlivening breath work, and heart-centering meditation. Now let's take the next step to healing by accessing and identifying the emotional toxicity from your past that is not serving you in the present.

Chapter Four

Parting the Veil: Identifying the Emotional Toxicity in Your Life

Dwell, O mind, within yourself;
Enter no other's home.
If you but seek there,
You will find all you are searching for.

— Sri Ramakrishna

It is your birthright to have a life of meaning and purpose. Whether or not the people in your life have consistently celebrated your incarnation, you deserve to celebrate your existence. Identifying any memory or belief that suggests the contrary is an essential step on the path to becoming free to love. It's important not to waste time, for although the celebration of life goes on forever, your personal invitation to the party lasts a brief lifetime.

How You Came to Be Who You Are

As you move along the path to emotional freedom, it is vital to recognize how you arrived at the place you are right now in your life.

Identifying the formative experiences and events from your past will help you more fully appreciate your present situation, giving you the awareness and understanding that will allow you to break free from deep-seated, unconscious thought patterns. From this place of conscious awareness and emotional freedom, you will be able to make the next chapter in your life more joyful, love-filled, and rewarding. As the ancient Buddhist text the Dhammapada tells us, "All that we are arises with our thoughts. With our thoughts we create the world." If, as a result of past experiences, you have an ongoing inner dialogue that is denying you love, this is the time to bring it into conscious awareness and create a new conversation.

It's important to understand how you develop a sense of self if you are to re-create one that supports emotional freedom and physical well-being. Knowing the four primary properties of the mind will enable you to consciously shift out of dysfunctional patterns of thoughts and feelings. The four functions of the ego mind are:

1) Registration
2) Labeling
3) Evaluation
4) Identification

As we go through life, our minds perpetually *register* experiences that enter into our awareness through our senses. We actually notice only a tiny percentage of events occurring around us, which is a good thing, for without our filters we would be perpetually overwhelmed by the ceaselessly flowing quantum soup of energy and information surrounding us.

As soon as we become aware of an experience, we immediately *label* the sensory impression by drawing upon our storehouse of memories.

You see a four-legged creature with a wagging tail and your mind produces the word *dog*. With a more refined vocabulary, your mind may generate the word *Rottweiler*. Look around you and notice how your labeling mind immediately assigns a word to every object of your attention – *phone, candle, door, plant,* and so on. The mind uses the same process to label actions and events, such as *breathing, smiling,* or *sleeping*. The labeling mind assigns every object to a vocabulary box to reinforce its sense of the familiar.

The *evaluating* aspect of the mind judges every experience as either desirable or undesirable. The primary criterion we use for this judgment of "good" or "bad" is whether or not what we perceive reinforces our outlook on the world. If it does, we label it "positive." If we perceive that something is in conflict with our point of view, we label it "negative."

Our prior experience with Rottweilers influences our present evaluation. For example, if you grew up with a loving pet Rottweiler, when you see one running around in a park without a leash, your assessment is likely to be positive. On the other hand, if your neighbors had a Rottweiler that barked at you whenever you walked past their home, you might evaluate the same free-running dog negatively.

The final stage of *identification* or *ownership* determines whether you make the experience, belief, feeling, thing, or relationship *yours*. Do you accept it or reject it? Does it become a part of you? Experiences that resonate with your established sense of self are more likely to be ingested and become a part of you; those that do not are more likely to be ignored, rejected, or filtered.

To better understand how the mental process of registration, labeling, evaluation, and identification applies in daily life, let's consider the scenario of meeting someone face-to-face on a first date. From the initial moment of connection, you begin registering information through your senses, and with every sensation you apply a label and make an evaluation: hairstyle – like; clothing style – don't like; low voice – like; cologne – don't like; food choice – like; etc. At some point during the course of the encounter, you will make a determination as to whether or not you might wish to integrate this person into your life. Will you see them again? Will you invite them back to your apartment? Will you become intimate? Will you live happily ever after?

Each person, of course, moves through these stages at different speeds depending upon their psychological nature and the potential "object" of acquisition. One person may make a snap decision about buying a new car they are attracted to (and believe reinforces their self-image), but take a long time before committing to a relationship. Someone else may easily fall in love at first sight, but spend days agonizing over which pair of shoes to buy.

Examining the core elements that originally created and continue to reinforce your self-image enables you to more consciously determine how new experiences influence your sense of self. Ultimately, what you determine to get under your emotional skin is a choice. The better you are at recognizing your emotional boundaries, the more successful you will be at making choices that allow nourishment in while keeping toxicity out.

Early Family Patterns

Our sense of self and the template for both our conscious and subconscious responses to situations, circumstances, and people are formed early in our development. Our personality develops to a substantial degree as we learn which aspects of our basic nature we need to express or repress in order to get our needs met. From birth on, we all have basic emotional needs for attention, affection, approval, and security.

As children, we were taught explicitly and implicitly which qualities, traits, beliefs, and behaviors would help us get our needs met – and which would not. If you were raised in a family of bankers and showed natural ability in art, you may not have received attention or approval for your talent. Your parents may have even openly criticized your interest in art as being frivolous in comparison with the "practical business" of banking. Your talent may have been stifled as you internalized the implicit lesson that pursuing art wouldn't fulfill your needs for approval, attention, affection, and security.

On the other hand, if your family valued artistic endeavors, your natural athletic ability may have been discouraged. Or you may have been born to parents who had an enormous enthusiasm for professional sports, but offered little encouragement for your interest in English literature.

In general, we associate the feelings of getting our needs met with the beliefs and values of those who meet them. In other words, we start believing that our parents' or caregivers' values must be right because they are espoused by the people who are meeting our needs. Over time, we take on those beliefs as our own.

Each of us has characteristics that we are generally comfortable expressing, and others that we keep buried. We claim title over those traits and beliefs that we have learned are valuable and deny ownership over those regarded as unworthy. The former become part and parcel of our ego or conscious self-image, while the latter are hidden in our unconscious or "shadow" self.

People identify themselves by the qualities and beliefs they've come to accept as true for them. When the average person is asked to define who they are, they will tell you what they spend most of their time thinking about. This usually translates into a chronicling of the

positions, possessions, relationships, and ideas with which they identify. When someone says, "I am a lawyer," they mean "I spend most
of my time thinking about the legal cases I am litigating." When a
woman says, "I am a mother," she implies, "I spend the bulk of my
day thinking about my children's school, food, clothing, laundry,
and well-being." If someone declares, "I am a Democrat" or "I am
a Republican," they are signifying, "I invest a major portion of my
thoughts into getting politicians elected who share my beliefs about
the role of government in people's lives." When a person says, "I am
an evangelical Christian," or "I am a Sunni Muslim," they are defining
themselves in terms of a core set of ideas that occupies their minds
and which they hold to be true.

Core Characteristics

Just as we define ourselves by our roles and our beliefs, our identity
is also delineated by the deeply held assumptions we have made about
our core characteristics, or who we are as a person. Although these
declarations of ownership over our essential qualities are usually more
obscure, each of us carries an inventory of beliefs about our self that
reflects the feedback we've received throughout our lives.

For example, based upon early conditioning, a woman may believe
and project to the world she is statuesque, charming, intelligent, and
powerful. If the same woman had been brought up in another home with
a different value system, she might instead have grown up to believe that
she is too tall, talkative, brainy, and pushy. Confidence in one context
may be interpreted as arrogance in another. Modesty in one setting may
be seen as timidity in another. In short, the *beliefs* we develop about our
core characteristics have a far greater impact on our sense of self than
the characteristics themselves.

During your developmental years, if you constantly received messages that devalued you, those negative judgments were woven into your identity. When children are told that they are useless, stupid, fat, loud, annoying, or clumsy, it is very difficult for them *not* to internalize these beliefs because their emotional boundaries are still developing and porous. Parents and caregivers who have challenges with their own self-esteem will often disown those uncomfortable traits and project them onto their family members. It is often easier to see characteristics in another person than in oneself. This ego defense protects one's ability to maintain self-importance or self-pity.

Parents who have unattainably high expectations for their children can also cause harm. If as a child you were expected to always be the best student, the star athlete, and perpetually perfect in every other way, your inability to achieve these goals consistently may have contributed to a sense of unworthiness. Even though your parents believed they were helping you reach your full potential, they created an environment in which, no matter how well you did, you never felt good enough, and thus you developed a deep-seated belief of inadequacy.

Witnessing Your Choices

As a result of these early subconsciously internalized beliefs about our core qualities and values, we engage in behaviors and express characteristics that reinforce our self-image. In one way or another, every choice we make declares to the world what we hold to be true and who we believe we are. Think about the choices you've made since you woke up this morning: the shampoo you used to wash your hair, your brand of toothpaste, the type of breakfast cereal you ate, and the radio station you listened to on the way to work reflect and express your sense of identity. The people with whom you associate, the places you go, and the mode of transportation you use to get there declare to the world your beliefs and values. The ego mind of a Hummer owner driving to a football game broadcasts a different message than that of a Prius driver going to a Humane Society fundraiser. Notice how spontaneously your judging mind becomes active just reading these examples. Despite any debate you might engage in about why your choice is better than someone else's, your ego mind is capable of rationalizing its point of view because it derives from and reinforces your self-image.

Step to Freedom

Spend the next twenty-four hours noticing the tendency of your mind to label and judge each experience you have. For example, listening to the weather report as you are getting dressed in the morning, you learn that it will be warm and sunny. Since this is consistent with your plan to meet a friend for breakfast at an outdoor cafe, you label the report "positive." As you drive to meet your friend, you become caught in a traffic jam. Since this delay is contrary to your needs, your mind labels it "negative." While searching for a traffic update, you tune in to a local news radio show. A reporter is interviewing a politician who is espousing beliefs about the military. You strongly disagree with her views and therefore label them as "negative." You switch to a radio station that is playing a favorite song, and your mind labels it "positive."

As you go through your day, observe how your state of being is affected by your relentless judging of situations, circumstances, people, and events over which you have limited or no control. Witness your tendency to judge, and *without judging the judge*, see if you can acknowledge that you are choosing one particular perspective out of many possible ones.

Observing your judging mind and reminding yourself about other possible perspectives will enable you to be more flexible and less frustrated by the differing viewpoints you encounter during the day.

Diving Within

Our core beliefs drive our thoughts, feelings, and choices. If these beliefs are unavailable to our conscious mind, they direct our life without allowing us to question the assumptions. Like a puppeteer pulling our strings from behind a curtain, these subconscious convictions compel us to feel, speak, and behave in ways consistent with the assumption, even if they are inconsistent with what our conscious mind tells us will bring us greater happiness, love, and well-being. In order to bring these hidden ideas and stories out of the shadows, we engage in a process of intuitive self-reflection.

It is first necessary to become aware of self-dishonoring characteristics, traits, and qualities to which you've given unwarranted power. Every child is worthy of unconditional love and acceptance but, sadly, many are deprived of their birthright. Disturbed parents, siblings, and peers project their pain and insecurities, and children suffer collateral damage in these covert wars. These pain-generated projectiles become lodged in the hearts and minds of people in the form of misunderstandings and mistaken beliefs. To free yourself from these toxic impressions, you need to part the veil and bring them into conscious awareness. To do so requires three elements: 1) Sensory Withdrawal/Retreat, 2) Evocative Questioning, and 3) Body Awareness.

Sensory Withdrawal / Retreat

In Chapter Two I introduced the concept of ama, which refers to the undigested residue of past experience. According to the principles of Ayurveda, biological beings have an innate digestive power or agni, which allows us to assimilate the experiences in our lives, extracting that which is nourishing and eliminating that which is not. If an experience overwhelms our ability to digest and assimilate it, we store the residue in our body or mind. Over time, this accumulated residue of past experiences inhibits our ability to fully metabolize what is happening in the present.

To access and begin the process of releasing emotional ama we need to reduce our intake of new experiences so that our agni can be directed to metabolizing leftovers. You can understand this principle on a physical level by considering how a low fat diet enables us to metabolize body fat accumulated from overindulging in the past.

Evocative Questioning

Your heart longs to be free of its burdens, and given the opportunity, will eagerly release the undigested pain, disappointment, betrayal, abuse, and neglect that is stifling its freedom to love. The process of accessing undigested emotional toxicity involves asking the right questions and listening to your heart for the answers. The answers are within you. You simply need to quiet your mind and listen for the responses that will guide you towards the love and happiness you deserve.

When you are ready to begin the self-questioning steps, find a comfortable place where you will not be disturbed. If possible, allow about an hour to focus on this exercise. Turn off your phones, let your children stay with your parents, and ensure that your pets are comfortable so they won't be scratching on your door or barking for your attention. Plan to spend time being quiet. Consider this process as a seduction by your inner self. The safer and more comfortable you can make the space, the easier it will be to become intimate with those hidden aspects of your being.

Put on some soothing music, light a few candles, and perfuse some calming aromatic essential oils. Spend a few minutes performing the heart-opening yoga poses and breathing exercises presented in the last chapter. Then settle into a comfortable chair or cushion on the floor and take about ten minutes to quiet your mind by using a meditation technique. In this quiet space, you will begin to ask the questions that can heal your heart.

Identifying Toxic Traits

Sit comfortably and take a few slow, deep breaths. Settle your awareness in your heart. Now ask yourself this difficult question:

What is wrong with me?

Although we spend much of our lives disguising and suppressing the answers to this question, this is your opportunity to access it. You carry negative self-judgments because you've accepted the opinions of others as legitimate. This is the time to challenge their validity. To help begin the process, look at the following list of traits that many clients have shared with me over the years, and see which ones provoke an emotional response in you.

Physical Characteristics	
I am too fat.	I am too thin.
I am too short.	I am too tall.
I am too dark.	I am too pale.
My hair is too curly.	My hair is too straight.

>>

My hair is too straight.	My teeth are too big.
My teeth are crooked.	My nose is too big.
My ears stick out.	My hands are ugly.
My feet are ugly.	My stomach sticks out.
My butt is too big.	My body is too straight.
My breasts are too big.	My breasts are too small.
I have cellulite.	My thighs are fat.
I am uncoordinated.	My penis is too small.
I have bad breath.	I have body odor.
I have bad skin.	I am a pig.
I am slow.	I can't sit still.

Mental and Personality Characteristics

I am stupid.	I am crude.
I am a smart aleck.	I am selfish.
I am a nerd.	I am boring.
I have no style.	I am foul.
I am rude.	I am insecure.
I am prissy.	I am a follower.
I am needy.	I am crazy.
I am timid.	I am useless.
I am incompetent.	I am hopeless.
I am clingy.	I am a loser.

I am untrustworthy.	I am a liar.
I am arrogant.	I am critical.
I am stuck-up.	I am lazy.
I am sarcastic.	I am worthless.
I am judgmental.	I am a mistake.
I am out of control.	I am annoying.
I am a control freak.	I am loud.
I am pathetic.	I have no talent.
I am disgusting.	I am withholding.
I am mean.	I too easily give in/put out.
I am narcissistic.	I am careless.

Body Awareness

Toxic emotions and beliefs have both mental and physical components. To fully identify the emotional ama you are carrying, you need to recruit the assistance of both your mind and body. As you consider various restricting beliefs and qualities you may have internalized, pay attention to the sensations in your body. The feelings that your body generates are like flares signaling that there is a buried memory or belief that wants to be discovered. Feeling your body while listening to your mind will ensure that you access the toxic residues of past experience so you can proceed on the path to healing your heart and healing your body.

Processing Your Inventory

Take out your journal and list the top tier of negative traits you have internalized. It should be easy for you to identify at least seven negative qualities you've accepted as yours. With time and attention, it will not be difficult for you to identify dozens. The best mind-set for approaching this process is understanding that for every negative quality we've accepted as true, a positive possibility hides just under the surface. Similarly, for every positive trait we accept as true, a negative trait is concealed in the shadows. Embracing our light and dark sides does not make us weak; it brings wholeness to our being.

Having identified the self-negating beliefs you have internalized, rank them, beginning with the most disturbing quality that has caused pain for you. Your list might look something like this:

1) I am a slob.
2) I am useless.
3) I am ugly.
4) I am a parasite.
5) I am an idiot.
6) I am self-centered.
7) I am unlovable.

Now consider the stories these traits reflect. Acknowledging the tales you've woven around these qualities begins to free you from the unconscious hold they have on you. Only then can you be free to experience happiness, vitality, love, meaning, and peace in your life.

Begin with the first trait on your list and ask yourself the following questions to help you recognize the roots and branches of the characteristic you have internalized. Write several paragraphs for each answer, recalling what you remember about this wounding.

1) When did I first hear this term applied to me? Who labeled me with this trait and what do I know about my tormentor?

2) What was happening in my life when this label was applied to me?

3) How has this label affected my sense of self and my relationships?

4) How has this trait affected my psychological and physical health?

5) Do I deserve to continue carrying the burden of this toxic trait in my heart? Do I deserve to be happy?

6) Has this belief, however painful, served me in any way?

7) How will recovering the power this trait has held affect my psychological and physical well-being?

One of my patients, Paul, a middle-aged lawyer with chronic bronchitis, hypertension, and persistent low back pain was ready to stop smoking cigarettes and reduce his use of pain medications. While processing his recent divorce, he wanted to begin making healthier choices. Paul identified "pathetic" as one of the top negative traits he was carrying. Accepting the validity of this label had caused him immeasurable anguish since childhood. Looking at the story woven around this quality, he wrote his responses to the questions above, revealing new insights that have helped him heal:

1) When did I first hear this term applied to me? Who labeled me with this trait and what do I know about my tormentor?

Paul remembered first being labeled as pathetic when he was about six years old. His mother had remarried an emotionally immature man who was resentful of any attention she gave to her young son. The stepfather, Jim, was often abusive, particularly when Paul's mom was not around. Paul's crying would further infuriate his stepfather, leading to threats such as, "If you complain to your mother about me, you pathetic brat, I'll kick both of you out of my house!"

Paul had not previously considered the life of his abusive stepfather, and he began to piece together the snippets of information he had registered over the years. Jim's father had been an angry man at whose hands Jim had suffered emotional and physical abuse. Drafted during the Vietnam War, Jim lost several close friends in combat. While in Vietnam, he began smoking opium and progressed for a while to heroin. Upon his return to the States, he drifted for several years until he found a job at an auto repair shop owned by a veteran he knew from his tour of duty. Post-traumatic stress combined with the responsibility of a wife and stepchild was simply too much for this wounded man.

2) *What was happening in my life when this label was applied to me?*

Paul recalled that after his biological father left the family, Paul's mother had moved them to live in the same town as her new boyfriend, who soon became her second husband. A lot had changed for Paul in a very short time – his father had left, he moved to a new home, started at a different school, and had to adjust to having a stepfather.

3) *How has this label affected my sense of self and my relationships?*

Paul internalized the notion that expressing sad emotions was a sign of weakness. Despite the overwhelming change he was being asked to adapt to, Paul became determined not to expose his feelings. Although he was not consciously aware of it at the time, Paul walled off a part of himself, because it was too costly to reveal his vulnerability.

Paul described his pattern of relationships as initial excitement and enthusiasm followed by progressively shutting down. With even a minimally critical comment from his partner, such as, "Do you really think your shirt goes with those pants?", Paul found himself withdrawing and becoming petulant. His first marriage ended after less than two years, because his wife complained that she was married to a ghost. He acknowledged that a major contributor to the demise of his second marriage was his increasing use of pain pills, which he consumed to anesthetize himself from his feelings of emotional incompetence, as much as to relieve his chronic backaches.

4) How has this label affected my psychological and physical health?

Paul acknowledged that regardless of how successful he appeared to others, he maintained an inner sense of insecurity. As a teenager he had learned that smoking cigarettes provided a temporary reprieve from his anxiety and reinforced his image as someone detached and immune to the opinion of others. He recognized that his pattern of using cigarettes as his steadfast "friend" was no longer serving him emotionally or physically.

5) Do I deserve to continue carrying the burden of this toxic trait in my heart? Do I deserve to be happy?

Paul had been in pain for so long that it hadn't dawned on him that he had a choice to create another reality. He was beginning to grasp how his acceptance of negative beliefs about himself had established patterns that were not serving him. The idea that he could relinquish self-damaging suggestions and replace them with self-celebrating ones was just beginning to seem like a possibility.

6)   Has this belief, however painful, served me in any way? How?

When we are encumbered with self-negating beliefs, it is difficult to see or accept that they are anything other than a drag on our vitality. However, it is common for an internalized negative trait to provide the fuel for a positive one. In Paul's case, he recognized that although his fear of being perceived as pathetic created serious challenges in his personal relationships, it also drove him to high levels of success in his career. His strong ambition derived much of its power from his need to prove his competence and his ability to control his emotions. Paul's challenge now was to reintegrate those aspects of his being that had been exiled. This was his path to emotional freedom.

7)   How will recovering the power trapped in this trait influence my psychological and physical well-being?

As Paul realized how his painful childhood experiences contributed to his emotional state and the habits he had developed to provide temporary relief, he acknowledged that he was still allowing his long-gone stepfather to cause him pain. He felt encouraged and inspired that by reclaiming the authority for his psychological and physical well-being, he could make the necessary health-promoting changes in his thoughts, feelings, and behaviors.

What's the Point?

There are two healing intentions underlying this exercise of identifying toxic beliefs. The first is to bring unspoken misunderstandings into the light. Self-denying internal beliefs thrive as long as they remain beneath conscious awareness. As a child, you may have feared a boogieman living under your bed. When you found the courage to shine a flashlight, you discovered a missing stuffed animal. In much the same way, fears residing in subconscious darkness lose their power when brought into the light – and often yield an unexpected reward.

The second intention of this process is to experience greater self-acceptance by embracing your inherent duality – the "good" and the "bad" inside you. Every human being can be generous and stingy, powerful and pathetic, open-minded and prejudiced. Acknowledging duality enables us to make conscious choices, rather than being subconsciously sabotaged. The frequent self-destructive behavior of public figures illustrates what happens when we deny our shadow self. A congressman attacking homosexuality with evangelical fervor is discovered to have a gay lover. A popular preacher, known for his fire and brimstone sermons on adultery, is exposed for his extramarital affairs. A holistic health guru cannot shake her secret tobacco habit. A Buddhist scholar lashes out when frustrated at his staff and family. Suppressed traits have the tendency to escape from their prison cells and cause harm.

Embracing qualities, traits, and characteristics over which you have felt shame and embarrassment frees up the emotional energy consumed in repression. This is because accepting these qualities allows the negative thoughts to be disconnected from their conditioned emotional responses. Once they are brought into the light of consciousness, you no longer have to unconsciously react in the same old way. Eleanor Roosevelt once said, "No one can make you feel inferior without your permission." In the acceptance of your duality, you regain the emotional power stolen by others and take a major step toward healing.

*

The work of emotional healing can be challenging, and I commend you for continuing on this path. I promise there is substantial treasure awaiting you.

Having identified the limiting toxic beliefs that have constricted your loving heart and harmed your body, you are now ready to complete the identification step by uncovering the stories of your life that have restricted your ability to be happy and healthy. You are one step closer to freedom.

Chapter Five

Digging Up the Past

Your grief for what you've lost
Lifts a mirror up
To where you're bravely working.

— JALALUDDIN RUMI

CHANGE IS THE ONLY CONSTANT IN LIFE — THE SOLE, STEADFAST friend we can trust. Yet we often resist it, holding on to memories and emotions that long ago ceased to serve us. Like stagnant water, torpid feelings breed disease. Toxic impressions left over from the past stem the heart's flow of loving and creative energy. Not only does this inhibit our joy and enthusiasm, it interferes with the natural healing forces in our body. Bringing awareness into emotional bogs allows fresh energy to clear the stagnation, providing creative opportunities for healing and transformation.

In the last chapter, through evocative questioning, you identified the key self-negating *beliefs* that generate emotional pain in your life The next step is to bring *experiences* from the past into focus so that healing can occur. Like body-mind-spirit archeologists, our goal is to unearth the artifacts of past events that limit our ability to be fully present and at peace with ourselves.

Bringing Your Stories to Light

People seeking emotional healing are usually motivated by a recent painful experience. They may have received a medical diagnosis they believe is related to life stress. They may be going through a difficult divorce or job loss. They may have recently experienced the passing of a loved one or are facing a challenging family relationship. Sometimes the motivation is the recognition that an unhealthy habit has become an addiction, and the individual wants to get to the source of the self-harming behavior. Most of us require a compelling reason to put time and energy into seeking emotional freedom and opening our heart.

We seem to need and usually have an explanation as to why we are not feeling well. Whether the problem is classified as predominantly emotional (depression, anxiety, irritability), physical (arthritis, cancer, ulcerative colitis), or somewhere in between (migraine headaches, irritable bowel syndrome, fibromyalgia), people have a story woven around their complaint. My experience is that even with the most prevalent of human ailments such as the common cold, most sufferers do not accept the purely biomedical explanation that it is caused by the transmission of a rhinovirus. Rather, we explain that the reason why we became sick was that we were working too hard, sleeping too little, eating poorly, or simply under too much stress.

If you ask someone in distress, "What's wrong?" they will usually begin telling you their story, chronicling the events that created the pain they are experiencing. Usually the story is about something that happened that they did not want to occur, or about something that they wanted to happen that did not. In either case, the event created an emotional wound that was not fully healed.

It's often apparent that they have been telling this story to themselves repeatedly, and they are now sharing aloud the dialogue they've been silently thinking for days, weeks, months, or even years. The narrative surrounding a need that has gone unmet or a boundary that has been violated describes the emotional wound, but in the retelling of the tale, the wound is often aggravated. In the Dhammapada, we're told,

> 'He abused me, he insulted me, he humiliated me, he took from me' – those who dwell on such thoughts will never be free from misery. 'He abused me, he insulted me, he humiliated me, he took from me' – those who relinquish such thoughts become free from misery.

Our challenge is to identify the misery-producing narratives so that we can reframe them in ways that allow our wounds to heal. In the next section, we will begin the process that will help you bring your own stories into the light.

Asking the Key Question

The intention of this step is to identify the landmark events that have shaped your emotional history. Spend a few minutes preparing your body through heart-opening stretching and breathing exercises to center yourself. Then, sitting comfortably, observe the inflow and outflow of your breath for a little while to quiet your mind. With awareness in your heart, ask yourself this important question:

> *What experiences from my past continue*
> *to create anguish for me in the present?*

Begin with the latest hurt. Perhaps you've been through a recent separation, have lost your job, or have become alienated from your family after a contentious inheritance battle. Provide your heart the opportunity to bring the emotional energy and information into your awareness as you replay the story and the feelings generated. Take a few minutes to document in your journal the significant points of the episode, noting what happened, when it happened, and who was involved.

Having identified the most recent pain-creating experience, take a few deep breaths, quiet your mind, and once again ask your heart to reveal another painful episode. Asking, *What experiences from my past continue to create anguish for me in the present?* evokes memories into conscious awareness. As one episode moves into consciousness, earlier pain-ridden experiences often follow the path from hidden to exposed. It is as if the human heart, sensing the chance to heal, wants to take advantage of the opportunity to bring painful stories to light. Be receptive to each memory that surfaces in your awareness and document the important details. Take a few minutes to journal the main points of each painful experience.

Continue this process of reaching back in time to identify significant episodes of emotional distress until you believe and feel you have accessed all major violations. In my experience, most people will feel they've uncovered their central painful stories if they perform this survey five to ten times.

As an example, here is a summary provided by Diana, a forty-one-year-old woman with recurrent stomach ulcers who recently attended a workshop at the Chopra Center. As you can see, she describes what happened in her seven most painful episodes.

1) Three months ago I learned that my husband of twelve years was having an affair with a colleague. I couldn't take the pain, and we are now legally separated and moving toward a divorce.

2) Six years ago I found out that my husband had had a brief affair with a client. My trust was broken, but we decided to work on keeping the marriage together.

3) Nine years ago my mother died. My older brother and I had dis-agreements over her estate that soured our relationship, which still remains distant and uncomfortable today.

4) Fourteen years ago, my fiancé broke off our engagement six weeks before our planned wedding. I still feel resentful and angry about both his actions and his timing.

5) My parents divorced when I was seventeen years old. I was a senior in high school and had trouble focusing on completing my college applications. I didn't get into the school I wanted and still wonder how my life might be different if they had waited a year before separating.

6) When I was a high-school sophomore, my best friend had a fling with a boyfriend with whom I had broken up only a week earlier. She didn't tell me directly until I confronted her with the rumors I was hearing. At first she denied that they were anything more than friends, but she eventually admitted that they had been flirting for months behind my back.

7) When I was eleven, my father was transferred to another city and we had to leave my home and friends. This was my second major move in three years, and I had just begun to feel comfortable with my new friends. I couldn't understand why my life had to be disrupted again.

Working It Through

Having identified your emotionally painful landmarks, the next step is to fully process each experience by asking deeper questions. I cannot overemphasize the value of journaling your responses rather than simply pondering them. Over many years, I've become convinced that journaling has a unique value of moving pain from the subconscious interior to conscious awareness, where it can be acknowledged and released. Here are the six key questions, which I'll explain in greater detail in the following pages.

1) What happened to me that caused the pain?

2) What was the context of this painful chapter in my life?

3) What feelings were generated?

4) What need was not met or what boundary was crossed that caused me pain?

5) What were the clues that I overlooked?

6) How was I served by denying the clues?

Each of these questions is designed to fully reveal the painful episode so that, once and for all, the emotional energy trapped in the story can be made available for healing and transformation.

1) What happened to me that caused the pain?

Tell your story, replaying the scenario from the moment the episode began to how it affects you now. How did it start? How did it unfold? Who was involved? What was said? What was done? Stick to the observable events, describing what happened as if you were a reporter giving a factual account of the episode. Describe only what an independent observer would have witnessed, withholding your interpretations and evaluations.

Let's return to the story of Diana, who was moving toward divorce after learning that her husband had had a second affair. Although she was in intense emotional pain, she used evocative questioning to learn as much as she could from this event. In response to the first question, Diana wrote:

I began suspecting my husband was cheating again when he stayed out late an increasing number of evenings each week. Most times, when I called him at the office, I would get his voicemail. His excuse for not calling me back for hours was that he was in intense business meetings from which he could not break away. When one evening I tried to reach him at the office, I was able to speak with his assistant, who told me he had left work hours earlier.

When he finally arrived home after 11 p.m., and I asked him how things had gone at work, he concocted an elaborate story about the late-night meeting he was stuck in. When confronted with the information I had received from his assistant, his explanation was so implausible that it would have been funny, had it not been so sad and infuriating. After hours of my confronting him about his obvious lying, he broke down and confessed that he'd been involved with a colleague at work for months. Despite his pathetic pleas to give him another chance, I knew that there was no going back.

2) What was the context of this painful chapter in my life?

If the pain goes back to early childhood, you may not remember a time without it, but most episodes do have a beginning. Envision your life before the experience. What was happening that set the stage for this episode? What components of the circumstances were outside of your control, and in what ways did your personal choices contribute to the episode? Becoming aware of the context provides insights into your role and responsibility in the experience.

An important note: Investigating your role and responsibility does not mean blaming yourself for events that were beyond your capacity to control. With experience, we learn that choices have consequences and we strive to make better ones. Looking back at events, you may recognize that had you known then what you know now, you would have responded differently. This is how wisdom develops. Considering the context of an experience helps you understand it better. With understanding, you can regain the power that was lost, given away, or stolen from you.

Here is an abbreviated version of Diana's discoveries about the context of her distress:

When our second child started first grade, I returned to work as a marketing manager. My long work hours put a strain on our marriage, which was still fragile as a result of my husband's earlier affair. I believed that since I was now making a significant financial contribution, my husband should assume a greater role in parenting. He expressed resistance to the change, arguing that because he was working as hard as ever in his job, he should not have to make major adjustments in his life. This friction fed my underlying resentment, leading me to withhold emotionally and physically. At the same time, my independence fueled his insecurities.

3) What feelings were generated?

Emotions are physical. We call them feelings because we *feel* them. No one relishes the pain generated when we fail to get our needs met, so we wall off uncomfortable feelings from our awareness. This fragmentation may be protective in the short run, but the longer-term consequences are emotional numbness and depression. Many physical symptoms – chronic pain, fatigue, digestive disorders, etc. – reflect the effects of pushing feelings out of awareness.

To heal your emotional wounds, you have to acknowledge the sensations in your body. As you are recalling experiences and relationships from the past, feel your body. Most people feel their emotions in the heart or gut. Sometimes feelings are perceived most intensely in the throat. People who defend against strong, uncomfortable emotions can develop back pain, neck pain, or headaches, for it can be easier to deal with a backache than heartache. If your goal is to eliminate the residues of emotional wounds, accepting your feelings is an essential component of genuine healing.

As you recount your stories, allow the sensations that accompany the narrative to enter into your awareness. Breathe into them. With each exhalation, allow the energy trapped in the feelings to circulate. While feeling your feelings, assign each emotion a name.

In labeling an emotion, use language that expresses as primitively as possible the sensations you are feeling. Words such as *sad, lonely, empty, angry, jealous, lost, resentful,* and *powerless* are authentic expressions of bodily sensations. Terms such as *neglected, rejected, betrayed,* and *disrespected* don't accurately express physical feelings; rather, they convey your interpretations of other people's intentions. When you resort to words that cultivate a victimization mind-set, your personal power and responsibility are squandered. As emphasized by psychologist Marshall Rosenberg in his insightful book *Nonviolent Communication*, the skill to use language that demonstrates your responsibility for your emotions restores your capacity to create a meaningful life. In fact, it's an essential requirement for emotional healing.

As Diana considered her experiences, she was able to identify a number of core feelings provoked by her seven painful memories:

1) My husband's recent affair: livid, terrified, empty

2) His affair six years ago: shocked, foolish, helpless

3) My mother's death and the fight with my brother: sad, disappointed, resentful

4) My broken engagement: furious, embarrassed, livid

5) My parents' divorce: angry, nervous, invisible

6) High school betrayal: embarrassed, empty, confused

7) Uprooting at age eleven: sad, empty, powerless

Reflecting on the emotions generated by the most recent painful event with her husband, Diana had the following insights:

When I discovered my husband was having another affair, I literally saw red. My immediate response was infuriation, and I admit I actually had the brief thought of buying a gun and shooting him and his girlfriend. For weeks, my feelings alternated between rage and sorrow.

As the initial shock wore off, I noticed other emotions brewing beneath the anger and grief. One was an awareness of disappointment with myself for not being strong enough to sever the relationship long ago. Another was a sense of responsibility for contributing to the situation through my not-so-subtle withholding of love and affection. Finally, I felt a small but genuine spark of exhilaration for the new future I could create.

4) What need was not met or what boundary was crossed that caused me pain?

All emotions derive from needs. Uncomfortable feelings arise when our basic needs for security, trust, attention, and caring aren't met, or when emotional or physical boundaries are crossed without permission.

We all require some sense of control, safety, and predictability in order to go about our daily lives. The threatened loss of a relationship, job, house, or health violates our sense of trust in the universe and activates primitive emotions of fear and anger. When something you thought was within your territory of influence leaves without your permission, or when something unwanted invades your domain, a hole in your sense of self is opened and life energy escapes. This wounding to your boundary of self generates feelings of distress.

See if you can identify how the situation or circumstance failed to meet your needs, or how it violated your boundaries of self. See if you can recognize how your pain resulted from realizing that something you believed was yours was no longer yours (e.g., a job, a relationship, a possession), or something that you did not believe was yours had become yours (e.g., a lawsuit, a diagnosis, a stepfamily's chaos).

Recognizing that your pain comes from an unmet need opens the possibility of identifying how you can consciously get your needs met. Recognizing that your pain is the result of a boundary violation opens the possibility of identifying how you can now establish healthy boundaries in your life. Recognizing that your past does not need to forever define your future will move you from a victimized state towards emotional freedom.

Reflecting on her painful story from the perspective of unmet needs, Diana wrote:

As I considered my pain in this context, my first thought was that my *need for <u>trust</u> was violated. I'd always imagined that when I married, my partner would be my best friend, but the betrayal that had taken place six years ago shattered my image. Beyond my need for trust, I realized that for years my needs for <u>attention</u> and <u>intimacy</u> had not been met. My husband seemed perpetually distracted by issues at work, and I had been consumed with raising the children, so there was little left to share when we were with each other. When I learned that "my intimacy" was going to another woman, I felt a hole ripped open in my heart. I really think our marriage died as a result of attentional starvation.*

5) What were the clues that I overlooked?

We tend to recreate scenarios that reinforce our earlier beliefs and patterns. Familiarity has an emotionally stabilizing influence even if the actual dynamics are unhealthy. For example, people raised in families with alcoholic parents often find themselves attracted to partners with drinking problems. Those with emotionally withholding parents often choose a mate with a similar emotional profile. People with controlling parents often gravitate to those who like taking charge.

I recently had a consultation with an intensive care unit nurse who reported a turbulent upbringing. As a child she shuttled back and forth between her divorced parents, who cohabited with and separated from a steady string of partners. She was repeatedly caught in the line of fire of emotional conflicts, and drama was a part of her daily life.

Her primary reason for seeing me was incapacitating migraine headaches that would usually occur on her first day off from work. In addition to her physical distress, she confessed that she felt emotionally empty and flat when she was not in the midst of the critical-care battlefield. Her personal relationships were routinely conflict loaded, and she noticed that despite the stress of her job, she actually became involved in arguments more frequently on her days off than when she was working. It was as if her baseline level of emotion was set at such a high intensity that she did not know herself if she was not in some crisis. Only when she became aware of this pattern could she effectively address her headaches.

Understanding how we tend to recreate contexts that remind us of prior experiences and bringing these patterns into awareness provide an opportunity to consciously choose something different. From a place of greater awareness, we begin to recognize clues as they present themselves, rather than being blindsided by painful situations. It is not uncommon for me to hear someone leaving a relationship say, "I knew from the beginning that this person was not right for me, but I kept ignoring the signs." The question, *What were the clues?* is designed to expand your awareness that you knew more than you probably wanted to acknowledge. Another way of asking the question moving forward is *What am I seeing that I don't want to see?* Using your past painful experiences to develop this skill can keep you from falling into emotionally hazardous territories. Hindsight is inevitably more precise than foresight, but learning from our experiences is how we gain wisdom, self-trust, and ultimately the freedom to love.

As Diana asked herself what clues she had chosen to overlook, she had the following insights:

I knew my husband had been unfaithful several times in his first marriage, but I accepted that his infidelity resulted from his immaturity. The first few years of our marriage were passionate and intense, but as soon as I became pregnant, he became distant. We had less intimacy and more arguments. Neither of us seemed very happy, and I was seriously considering leaving when

I learned of his first affair. Fearing the effects of a divorce on my children, I decided to stay in the marriage, at least until the kids were older.

After six months of counseling, we established a new rhythm. My husband was focused on his work, routinely expressing his plans to acquire enough wealth so that neither of us would have to work. On his frequent business trips, he was usually diligent about calling home, although occasionally he was unreachable for hours.

He explained his recent newfound enthusiasm for working out at a fitness club several days a week by saying that it helped him dissipate stress from his job. His frequent texting on his PDA only aroused my concern when he almost reflexively pulled it away a few times when I glanced over his shoulder while he was typing.

On these occasions, I had two conversations going through my mind. One said, "After what we went through last time, and the promises he made if I would stay, he couldn't be stupid enough to risk everything again." The other voice said, "If he is stupid enough to have another affair, I don't really care enough anymore to fight it."

6) How was I served by denying the clues?

Because we are multidimensional beings, there will be times when one part of us conflicts with another. Our more rational, wise self wants to lose weight to be healthier, while a more indulgent, childlike part of us wants to eat that piece of strawberry cheesecake. Our entrepreneurial adventure-seeking self wants to quit our job and start a new business, while our more conservative voice cautions us to stay put and maintain the financial security of working for an established company. Our emotional heart is adept at overlooking and denying the reasons why our love might better be invested in another relationship than one causing us heartache. Asking, *How is this denial serving me?* can dispel some of the fog of attachment and keep you faithful in your pursuit of emotional freedom.

Diana recognized that although her marriage was not a reliable source of emotional nourishment, she was willing to stay in it for the sake of her children and to avoid taking on more responsibility than she believed she could handle. She wrote:

> *Putting on a face of stability at home served me at work, where many colleagues marveled at my ability to competently manage marriage, family, and job. I was also unwilling to deal with my mother's disapproval. I realized how well I had been able to justify not rocking the boat, or perhaps to state it more accurately, how unwilling I was to acknowledge that the boat was already rocking and about to capsize.*

Step to Freedom

I believe in the fractal theory of relationships, which states that everything that *will* be revealed in a relationship is present from the first encounter. Although in our quest to connect, we have the tendency to ignore obvious clues, in retrospect we can usually recognize that the signs were there from the beginning.

Consider a relationship you had that did not work out. Divide a piece of paper with a vertical line. On the left side, list those qualities that you would consider desirable. On the right side, list those you'd label undesirable. Now that you have the benefit of time and experience, look at all the so-called negative qualities and see how many you saw but were unable or unwilling to acknowledge at the time, because your need to connect with another person obscured your connection with yourself.

Contemplate the fact that each of us has qualities we want to show the world, and those we try to keep hidden. As you consider yourself, notice that characteristics buried in your shadow do not disappear; they simply go underground.

Healthy relationships do not and cannot require people to be only good. They do call for us to be committed to acknowledging and integrating both our light and dark sides. This is the path to wholeness and acceptance.

Writing Your Story

It's tempting to read the stories in this book or hear how other people work through their pain and believe that you are benefiting. However, I have learned that thinking through an emotional challenge is not as healing as taking the time to put your thoughts and feelings into writing. It is as if by getting the words onto paper, the emotionally painful experience loses its grip on your heart.

Please take the time now to focus on each of your painful experiences from the past and write your own responses to the six questions:

1) What happened to me that caused the pain?

2) What was the context of this painful chapter in my life?

3) What feelings were generated?

4) What need was not met or what boundary was crossed that caused me pain?

5) What were the clues that I overlooked?

6) How was I served by denying the clues?

Write until you have nothing left to say about each experience. If you sense that there is more to reveal but have difficulty accessing the information, do another round of heart-opening yoga poses and breathing exercises. Sometimes going for a walk while staying in a state of intuitive self-reflection can bring hidden memories to the surface. Writing with your nondominant hand can also reveal surprising insights, which come from tapping into different parts of your brain that can access memories you buried long ago. If you stay with this process, you will reach a state of clarity. Keep going until you get there. As you bring your painful stories into the light of awareness, the pain, resentment, and regret that have kept you in bondage begin to loosen their grip, moving you another step closer to the freedom of self-love and acceptance.

*

This completes the identification step. Through your diligent work, you have now brought into your awareness the toxic beliefs and painful experiences that have limited your capacity for happiness and health. In the act of identification, you have already begun to mobilize emotional ama from your body, heart, and mind.

In the next chapter you will complete the mobilization process and proceed to the fourth step of release. Even though this process is challenging, I encourage you to stay with it. You are getting closer to healing your emotions and healing your body.

Chapter Six

Releasing Your Pain

What do sad people have in common?
It seems they have all built a shrine to the past
And often go there and do a strange wail and worship.
What is the beginning of happiness?
It is to stop being so religious like that.

— HAFIZ

How do you let go of the pain from your past? That is the central question for those seeking emotional freedom. Despite your intention to release the pain, it may seem at times as if the pain is unwilling to release *you*. If you've stayed with the process to this point, you are now ready to liberate your heart from the emotional tyranny that has been holding it hostage. Conscious movement, energizing breath work, and intuitive self-reflection have helped you prepare, identify, and mobilize the toxic residues of limiting beliefs and heart-wounding experiences. It is now time to fully mobilize and release the painful charge that has been trapped within your heart.

Letting go doesn't mean that you will lose your memories or forget your lessons. Rather, you will release from your mind and body the festering pain that keeps you from living and loving with freedom and clarity.

Drain Your Pain

The goal of these mobilizing and releasing procedures is to drain your pain without causing harm to you or those around you. The first step in this process is to share your stories with someone who can listen compassionately without attempting to "fix" your problem. Ideally this is a best friend or trusted family member who is willing to support an approach that serves you.

If you do not currently have someone in your life who meets this requirement, I encourage you to find a counselor, therapist, or clergy member who can play this role for you. There is immeasurable value in telling your story to another human being who will listen with love, without assuming responsibility for your anguish or trying to rescue you. As I've consistently observed in the pair work participants do at workshops, a caring person can be just as effective as a healthcare professional. However, if there is no one with whom you can share your intimate stories and feelings, I will guide you through a visualization exercise that can serve this purpose. The essential component of this step is to give *verbal* expression to your story. Journaling has the value of identifying and mobilizing toxic emotional residue. Communicating the story aloud fulfills the mobilization stage and begins the process of releasing.

Sharing Your Story

Confession is good for the heart as well as the soul. The painful secrets you hold within fester and stagnate, breeding sorrow. Your inner and outer worlds mirror each other. To have freedom in your life, you must create freedom at your core. To liberate yourself from self-denying beliefs, you must open your heart and release the pain that has kept you closed off from yourself and others.

I never cease to be amazed at how often my patients, sharing their stories of early boundary violations, tell me they've never told anyone their secrets before. Children treated inappropriately invariably sense the transgression is wrong, but frequently choose not to reveal it to a parent or caregiver, often for reasons that are difficult to articulate. They may have worried that they weren't going to be believed, been fearful of the consequences, or felt guilty that they in some way contributed to the violation. There are, of course, times when an abuser intentionally intimidates the victim, but even without explicit threat, children frequently barricade their pain and shame behind a wall of silence.

Sadly, people wounded early in life often have difficulty cultivating intimate relationships. Sensing inner damage, they are afraid to expose their vulnerabilities, believing that they are different and will be rejected by others. If you can relate to this pattern, this negative cycle must end if you are to rejoin the life stream of love.

Working with a Listening Partner

If you have someone willing to serve as your witness, share the following instructions with your partner. Although most people are not naturally great listeners, anyone can be taught. Explain to your partner that the best way to support you is by following this simple direction:

> *You serve me best by listening attentively as I tell you*
> *my story, without attempting to fix my problem.*

The goal of this process is to bring movement to constricting emotions and begin releasing them. Telling your story without the need to defend or explain best supports this process. Therefore, the type of feedback that occurs in normal conversations is not encouraged during this stage. Whether you are revealing your story to a friend or verbalizing aloud on your own, the point is to say what happened without being interrupted.

Seeing your personal story within the context of the greater human drama expands your perspective and reduces the pain that comes from taking things personally. The challenges we all face in managing our relationships with the world provide the raw substance for the myths and legends shared by every culture on earth. Core human themes of unrequited love, jealousy, betrayal, loss, exploitation, and neglect are the basic elements for stories told across time and space. The tales of Greek and Roman mythology, the comedies and tragedies of Shakespearean plays, the stories of the Bible, the legends of the Vedic Puranas, and the dramas of television soap operas remind us that our individual tragedy is a variation on the theme of human calamity. Your story and my story are threads in the fabric of life and love, dyed with our anguish and our redemption.

This is the time to give expression to your stories – to communicate the details that were revealed in prior chapters through intuitive self-reflection. Sitting with your listening partner in a comfortable position, share your first painful experience, including each of the aspects you wrote about in your journal:

1) Communicate the context of the painful experience.

2) Communicate the full range of feelings generated by this experience.

3) Communicate your unmet needs.

4) Communicate the clues available to you that you denied.

5) Communicate how your denial served you.

When you have shared your story from these five perspectives, ask your partner to respond by saying the following three phrases to you:

Thank you for sharing your story and feelings with me.
I'm sorry for the pain you experienced.
I offer you my love as a balm for your wounded heart.

Using this framework, share each of the painful experiences you've identified from your past and, after each five-part sharing, ask your listening partner to respond as above. This ritualized way of expressing your pain may sound contrived, but I encourage you to follow this script. I've witnessed the power of this process and want you to experience the benefits for yourself.

Envisioning Your Inner Healer

If you are doing this process on your own, take a few minutes to quiet your mind by practicing breathing awareness and meditation. Using your power of imagination, envision yourself in a place of safety and beauty. Perhaps it's a lush mountain ridge overlooking a verdant valley, a tropical beach with azure water lapping up against white sand, or a natural hot springs in an old-growth forest.

Upon arrival at your sacred place, imagine a powerful tree of wisdom with its roots in the earth and its branches reaching to the sky. Envision a being of love and compassion sitting beneath this tree. It may be a religious figure such as Jesus, Moses, Buddha, or Krishna. It may be a wise old man or woman, or perhaps a celestial being of light. Visualize sitting in the presence of this divine being and allow their serenity to fill your heart.

In the same way that you would express your story to a human being sitting next to you, communicate to this sacred archetypal entity the experiences and episodes that caused you pain. With your eyes closed, share your painful stories, speaking aloud as if you were there with this being in person.

After each story, imagine your inner healer saying these three statements:

Thank you for sharing your story and feelings with me.
I'm sorry for the pain you experienced.
I offer you my love as a balm for your wounded heart.

Confessions of Your Humanity

Connecting and sharing with other people is essential to emotional and physical health. Early in my career I read an article in an anthropology journal entitled "Voodoo Death," which described what happens in certain cultures when an individual violates a major tribal rule. The shaman or witch doctor is called in to pronounce the person "dead." From that moment forth, the violator is completely shunned by the community. The stress of this total alienation resulted in documented cases of death within days to weeks. The person literally dies of loneliness and fear. As this article underscored, most people need human connection to live and thrive.

Your emotional heart is the expression of millions of years of evolution. For our species to survive, we had to adapt to changing and often dangerous environments. Since we are more physically vulnerable than most predators, we learned to band together in families and tribal communities to enhance our likelihood of surviving a treacherous world.

Through these relationships, we learned how to meet our personal needs while supporting others in our group to meet theirs. Survival depends on maintaining a delicate balance between the needs of the individual and the needs of the tribe. Managing these boundaries continues to be a major challenge for the human species.

When you've experienced emotional pain that comes from unmet needs or boundary violations, your sense of connection to the whole is threatened, resulting in anxiety, frustration, and depression. The physiological shifts that accompany these psychological states sow the seeds for physical illness. However, by reestablishing breached boundaries and reconnecting through healthy relationships, the mind and body can heal.

Loving relationships play a crucial role in the healing response throughout the stages of life. Premature babies develop more rapidly if cuddled lovingly, patients with heart attacks recover faster if they feel loved by their spouses, and people with autoimmune illnesses or cancer respond to loving interactions with healthier immune responses. In fact, numerous scientific studies provide evidence that loving relationships are a vital ingredient in creating physical health. If you are interested, a selection of these studies is provided in the Appendix.

Getting to the Essence of Your Pain

The next step on your path to healing prepares you to distill your painful stories in preparation for releasing their toxic influence on your life. To do this, we will use a powerful concept from India's ancient Vedic tradition – the *sutra*. As you continue your healing process, it will be important to understand what a sutra is and how it works, so let's take a brief foray into history to explore the essential meaning and purpose of sutras.

Passing Down Wisdom

Before the development of writing, the knowledge of various wisdom traditions was passed down from generation to generation through oral transmission. The style of knowledge-sharing developed by the Vedic sages thousands of years ago is known as *sutra*. *Sutra* is a Sanskrit word that translates as "thread" or "stitch." It is related to the words *suture* and *ligature*, which mean "holding together."

In the Vedic tradition, a sutra is a word or phrase that holds together a deeper or more expanded idea or story. Students were able to memorize sutras and retain the full understanding of the wisdom they contained. For example, in the classic yoga text, the Yoga Sutras of Patanjali, the Sanskrit sutra *yogah cittavritti nirodhah* (which means "yoga is the progressive quieting of thought forms in the mind") encapsulates the entire philosophy of yoga in three words. Entire treatises have been written about this short phrase, expanding upon its meaning and offering various interpretations.

So what do sutras have to do with emotional healing? They are the cords that bind your painful memories, thoughts, and emotions, holding you in bondage to the past. Our goal in this step of the healing process is to identify the mental threads that have stitched emotional pain into the fabric of our being. To identify your emotional sutras, refer again to the painful stories you evoked in Chapter Five in response to the question, *What experiences from my past continue to create anguish for me in the present?* You shared these stories with your listening partner, communicating the event, the feelings they generated, and their short- and long-term influences on your sense of self and your relationships. As you review what you wrote in your journal, find a word or short phrase to serve as the sutra for each painful experience. Think of these expressions as chapter titles or headlines that quickly bring to heart and mind the story they represent.

I recently consulted with a young woman whose story may help you better understand the process of finding a sutra. Anne had been suffering with chronic fatigue for several years. Although she was currently in a good marriage and adored her four-year-old daughter, she was incapacitated by her inability to sustain more than an hour of daily activity. Despite numerous medical evaluations by both conventional and alternative practitioners, and a plethora of explanations (including mercury toxicity from her dental fillings, food allergies, spinal subluxations, yin deficiency, and so on), her quality of life was deteriorating.

In her healing work, Anne accessed early memories of watching her raging father hurting her mother and older sister. Even as a young girl she received excessive spankings, and she remembered hiding in bed under the covers when her father came home from work, hoping he would not discover her.

As she recalled these years of emotional and physical abuse, she accessed the residual pain, anger, loneliness, and fear that she had buried deep in her unconscious many years ago. Anne found that the sutra that encapsulated her childhood experience was *extinguishable*, a word expressing the deep sense that her life was so insignificant that it could be easily snuffed out by others. This is the essence of a sutra – it is a word or phrase that captures a much bigger story.

As you review each of your seven most painful experiences, identify the key word or phrase – the suture or stitch – that holds the painful memory together. When you have completed your review of your stories, you will have identified seven sutras, representing the major obstacles to healing your heart.

Loosen the Grip of Toxic Beliefs

To complete the preparation for release, look at the seven (or more) undesirable traits you discovered in your intuitive self-reflection in Chapter Four. Again, ask your listening partner to participate in this next process with you. Your instructions to your partner are as follows:

1) I will express to you a trait I have been holding in my heart that reinforces a lack of value.

2) When I reveal this trait to you, I want you to mirror it back to me.

3) I will then repeat the same undesirable quality a second time.

4) You will again mirror it back to me.

5) You will then tell me, "I love you regardless of this quality."

To understand how this process works, imagine that one of the negative beliefs you've identified is that you are a slob. Closing your eyes, consider again for a few moments how that one toxic belief has affected your life. Then, holding hands with your listening partner, look into each other's eyes, and have the following dialogue:

You say:	*I am a slob.*
Your partner mirrors back:	*You can be a slob.*
You repeat:	*I can be a slob.*
Your partner mirrors back:	*You can be a slob.*
	And . . . I love you anyway.

Using this structure, go through each of the seven traits you identified, sharing the quality, receiving the feedback, sharing the quality again, and receiving the feedback and unconditional acceptance from your partner.

If after the first round you sense that you still have a residual emotional charge about any of the traits, repeat the process until you completely release the charge for all the negative beliefs. Through this revealing exercise, you will find that the undesirable quality or self-defeating belief loses its hold on you. Through your conscious "owning" of the trait, embarrassment and vulnerability dissipate.

Accessing Your Inner Healer

If you are doing this process on your own, you can use your power of imagination to gain the benefits. Again, quiet your mind through breathing awareness meditation and envision your sacred place, where your symbolic being of love and compassion resides. Imagine receiving unconditional acceptance from this loving being as you confess the uncomfortable traits you've identified.

Say each trait aloud with your eyes closed and visualize your sacred being mirroring it back to you. Hear them offer their unconditional love for you, despite and because of your willingness to acknowledge a quality you've judged to be negative. Declare and embrace the trait until it has lost its power over you.

Cellular Release

Your body is your subconscious mind, storing memories through a code that transcends language. Emotions carry energy and information, which you can access by attending to the sensations your body generates. In his novel *Jitterbug Perfume*, author Tom Robbins declares that there are only two mantras in life: *yum* and *yuck*. These are the mantras of the heart, informing us of our current inventory of met or unmet needs. The human mind is adept at ignoring emotional pain until it builds to the point where it can no longer be discounted.

Accessing your stored pain through intuitive self-reflection and beginning the release process in your work with a partner or guided visualization has prepared you for the next step of physical releasing. The process I share in the next section is pivotal in making a quantum leap from old patterning to new possibilities. Again, reading about it is not the same as doing it. You won't get the benefits if you don't do each step, so I encourage you to just do it!

Making Your List, Checking it Twice

Let's review. If you've been doing the work, you now have identified seven experiences that have contained painful memories for you, and seven traits or beliefs about yourself that have limited your sense of value. Lay them out on one page so that you can see the words that tell the story that has been directing your emotional life. It might look something like this:

Painful Stories
1) My husband's recent affair: *Violation*
2) My husband's first affair: *Betrayal*
3) My mother's death: *Emptiness*
4) My broken engagement: *Foundation shaking*
5) My parents' divorce: *Powerless*
6) My high school betrayal: *Embarrassment*
7) My uprooting at age eleven: *Invisible*

Painful Traits
1) *Slob*
2) *Useless*

3) *Ugly*

4) *Parasite*

5) *Idiot*

6) *Self-centered*

7) *Unlovable*

The next step is to take a clean sheet of paper and write the seven sutras that encapsulate your painful experiences and messages you've internalized. Then write the seven negative traits you've identified. This is the distillation of the suffering in your life – all of your struggles condensed into fourteen words or short phrases on one page.

You are now ready to perform a ritual to declare to your heart, mind, body, and soul your willingness and readiness to relinquish the painful charge this information has been holding for you. It's now time to release the barriers to healing your heart.

Rituals of Release

As the author of your life script, you are responsible for consciously writing a new story. This ritual declares both to the world and to yourself, *This old chapter is ending. A new chapter is beginning.* This ritual is designed to put a big *The End* on your old story. You've paid your dues. It's time to heal.

First you will need to find a place in a natural environment near your home where you can be alone and free from distractions. The ideal spot is next to an ocean or on a lake shore. Other possibilities include a mountain ridge, the banks of a river, or the edge of a meadow or forest. The essential thing is to find an open space where you can be alone with your thoughts and feelings without having to worry about someone observing you.

When you've decided on a natural environment that feels comfortable to you, set aside a couple of hours so that you can fully focus your attention on the release ritual.

The Process

Sit quietly with your eyes closed for a few minutes, absorbing the sounds, sensations, and fragrances that surround you. Once you are confident that you have chosen the appropriate space, gather up at least fourteen rocks or stones. These will serve as your releasing vehicles.

Now stand at the edge of the ocean, lake, or meadow with your eyes closed, holding the first rock to your heart. Bring into your awareness the first sutra that encapsulates an emotionally painful experience. Allow the story to play again in your awareness, while holding the intention to "load" the rock with your painful feelings. This will usually take about ten minutes. The purpose of this step in the ritual is to separate the emotional charge from the facts of your story.

When you feel the rock is fully "charged," throw it away from you with all the force you can muster. Scream, shout, or swear at the top of your lungs to support the cathartic release of the emotional ama you've been carrying. The only restriction in this exercise is to be certain that you do not harm yourself.

After you have released the first rock, center yourself in your heart and be present with your emotions. If tears rise to the surface, allow them to flow without resistance. When you feel that you have come back to your center, bring into your awareness the sutra that captures the essence of the second painful experience you have accessed. Hold another rock to your heart and repeat the process, replaying the painful scenario on the screen of your mind while "charging" the rock with your distressing feelings. After about ten minutes of telling yourself the story, heave the rock into the ocean, canyon, or wherever you happen to be, using your body and voice to release.

Continue the ritual until you have processed all seven of your most painful experiences. Most people find that there is diminishing charge as they move down the list. Still, do not short-circuit the process by thinking, *Okay, I get it,* and then simply tossing away the remaining stones. In order to experience maximum relief, you must perform the whole ritual for each memory, even if it requires stretching beyond your comfort zone. Don't shortchange yourself! This is your opportunity to claim your emotional freedom.

Releasing Dishonoring Beliefs

In the same way that you accessed and released the emotional charge of painful experiences, process each of your undesirable beliefs. Holding a rock to your heart, bring the first negative quality or belief into your awareness. As you review the story woven around that trait, envision extracting the pain and transferring it to the rock. When you feel the separation between the story and your emotions, release the stone with passion, using your body and your voice. Take your time recalling, discharging, and releasing each trait.

Step to Freedom

During each workshop, I ask participants to make a number of commitments – to show up, to take responsibility, to be honest, to care, to express, to move, and to stretch. I ask the same of you. Having read this chapter, it is now time for you to act. Take your list of painful experiences and uncomfortable traits and perform the releasing ritual. In order to be without sin . . . you must cast all the stones.

After completing the releasing rituals, be gentle with yourself and take it easy for the rest of the day, allowing your mind and body to digest what you've experienced. Settle into your new state of being. Many people feel exhilarated after this releasing ritual, but it is not uncommon to feel exhausted and depleted. Even an uncomfortable pattern of thinking and feeling reinforces a sense of self by its familiarity. If you are wondering, *Who am I if I am not this story I've been telling?* I assure you that the emptiness you're now feeling will become the space into which love, vitality, and purpose will soon flow. Get some rest, listen to soothing music, take a warm bath, and applaud yourself for the great work you've accomplished in pursuit of becoming free to love.

You've now crossed the threshold of healing and cannot return to your previous heart-constricted state. Having freed yourself from the imprisoning effects of limiting stories and beliefs, you have cleared space in your heart for more love, fulfillment, and grace. From an Ayurvedic perspective, this is the point at which you are the most receptive to the healing benefits of rejuvenation and rest. You've released the emotional toxins of the past and are now ready to nourish yourself with expanded love and energy.

Chapter Seven

Rejuvenating with Love

Where there is hatred, let me sow love.

— SAINT FRANCIS OF ASSISI

IN THE KATHA UPANISHAD, AN ANCIENT SCRIPTURAL TEXT FROM INDIA, a young boy, Nachiketa, embarrasses his father during a public ceremony. His father is so mortified that he curses his son with the Vedic equivalent of "Go to hell," shouting in his rage, "I send you to death!" Nachiketa accepts the expulsion, and using his meditative skills, transports himself to the abode of Yama, the King of Death.

When he arrives, Nachiketa is told by Death's aides that Yama is on a business trip rounding up souls from a recent epidemic and will not return for several days. Nachiketa plants himself at Death's door, meditating with complete self-control. When Yama arrives three days later, he is informed by his assistants that Nachiketa has demonstrated a level of composure rarely seen at the threshold of death. Yama arouses Nachiketa from his trance, apologizes for the poor manners shown by his unsophisticated assistants, and offers the boy compensation for keeping him waiting. Nachiketa immediately requests that his father forgive him if he returns to the land of the living. Yama assures him that when his father sees him alive and well, he will unconditionally forgive him.

This ancient story offers a powerful message: We navigate the path to emotional freedom through forgiveness. Resentments, grievances, and regrets disturb our peace and make it impossible to be fully present. A similar message is contained in the Egyptian myth of Anubis, a god who meets us at our death and weighs our heart against the feather of justice. If our heart is lighter than the feather, we are liberated for eternity. If, however, our heart has become heavy with the burden of carrying resentments and regrets, it is eaten by Ammit, god of destruction.

Getting to Forgiveness

When someone's actions create pain for us, it is natural to engage in an inner conversation of resentment. The mind replays the offense, repeating the stories over and over. *My wife betrayed me. My father destroyed my trust. My partner didn't come through for me.* And so on. The dialogue of blame disturbs the peace of both mind and body. The Buddhist text the Dhammapada reminds us how important it is to free ourselves from the toxic conversations that preoccupy our mind:

> *Hatred can never put an end to hatred; love alone can.*
> *This is the eternal truth.*
> *People forget that their lives will soon end.*
> *For those who remember, quarrels come to an end.*

When we consider how it is possible that someone could behave in ways that create anguish for us, it is useful to recognize that their choices reflect the story they've been living. Although they may not always be good ones, there are reasons why people sometimes make choices that hurt others. More often than not, it is because, given their existing level of awareness, they were unable to entertain other options to get their needs met in ways that wouldn't create pain for another. Even the most seemingly incomprehensible tragedies caused by terrible acts of violence become more understandable as we recognize the context of what happened. Consider the following examples.

A young boy was routinely beaten by his father. Two of his brothers and a sister died in childhood. The boy's father died when he was fourteen, and his mother died when he was eighteen. He did poorly at school and was homeless by the time he was twenty. He grew up angry and unloved. It is not a big stretch to imagine that had Adolf Hitler's early life been more loving and supportive, he would have been incapable of perpetrating his crimes against humanity.

Another boy's father died while his mother was pregnant with him. A few months later, the boy's brother also died. His mother attempted suicide by throwing herself in front of a bus, and when that was unsuccessful, she would pummel her abdomen with her fists. She is quoted as saying, "After losing my husband and child, what good can this baby do for me?" When her son was born, she would have nothing to do with him and sent him away to live with an uncle. Again, it is not hard to envision that had his life begun differently, Saddam Hussein might not have become a brutal dictator, responsible for the deaths of thousands.

We are, of course, responsible for our choices, and there are abundant examples of people who, despite growing up in environments of abuse or deprivation, go on to live magnificent lives of service and compassion. Our past does not have to define our future. Still, understanding the experiences of others helps us move towards forgiveness, which is necessary if we are to fully heal and be free to love.

Creating a Story of Understanding

Consider a person in your life whom you associate with painful feelings. It might be an ex-spouse, an offensive boss, an abusive stepparent, or a best friend who betrayed your trust. Contemplate the interactions you've had with this person who created pain for you. For the purpose of freeing your heart from the constriction caused by resentment, shift your focus from what happened to you to what was happening in the life of the person who caused your pain.

Accessing what you know about this individual's life, begin constructing their biography. The goal is to understand how the person who caused you pain could do what they did. Journal the details you are aware of, and then fill in the blanks using your imagination. Here are some questions that can help you with this step:

- What do you know or imagine about the emotional and physical health of their parents or caregivers?

- Was the individual who caused you pain planned and wanted by their parents?

- How was this person treated as a baby and young child?

- How did their family members and peers relate to them?

Take your time to construct a biography that helps you understand how this person became someone who was capable of doing the things that have caused you (and most likely others) pain.

Rachel's Story

Rachel, a recent participant at a *Free to Love* workshop, had been carrying tremendous pain and anger towards her stepfather, Jack, for emotionally and physically abusing her as a child. For years she had been dealing with two disabling health conditions: irritable bowel syndrome and fibromyalgia. Despite seeking help from gastroenterologists, rheumatologists, naturopathic doctors, and Traditional Chinese Medicine practitioners, she had been able to achieve only limited relief from her symptoms. Although she had gained some benefits from antidepressant and sleeping medications, Rachel attributed her weight gain and difficulty concentrating to side effects of those drugs. Her relationships were similarly distress-ridden, for she invariably chose men who picked up on and reinforced her low self-esteem.

During the workshop, Rachel performed the rituals of identifying, mobilizing, and releasing the pain associated with her painful story, but she still felt the residue of the boundary violations. She said, "I feel there is a hole in my heart through which my life energy is leaking."

Rachel initially resisted the idea of looking at her stepfather's life and seeking an explanation for his behavior. "The man was a monster," she said, "and there's no way I could ever understand how he could have treated me the way he did." However, since all of her previous attempts to get relief from her disabling conditions had failed, she gradually became willing to at least test the process of understanding. With support and encouragement, she began recalling fragments of information about her stepfather's life that she had long ago buried. She also became motivated to call her mother and find out more details about him.

Through talking with her mom, Rachel learned that Jack's father had been an alcoholic who physically abused his son before ultimately abandoning the family. Jack had been small and skinny as a child and was frequently bullied while growing up in Queens, a borough of New York. Shortly before joining the Army, he married for the first time, but while on a tour of duty he learned that his wife was having an affair and was divorcing him. Jack began drinking heavily while he was serving in the military, and he continued to struggle with alcohol after he was discharged.

As the painful stories of her stepfather's life emerged from the shadows, Rachel found herself weeping for the pain that was woven through his, her mother's, and her own life. Through this understanding, she began to feel a trickle of forgiveness that had previously been unavailable to her. Over time, she was able to see that her stepfather's abuse had had nothing to do with who she was but rather was the expression of a man whose heart was filled with pain and self-loathing. She stopped seeing herself in his distorted mirror and began repairing her self-worth, her health, and her ability to love.

Intentions into Actions

As you craft a story of understanding, you will experience the seeds of compassion sprouting in your heart. The life-damaging actions that created suffering are unacceptable, and yet recognizing that people are doing their best given the resources available to them at the time can help you become free from the imprisonment of your emotional turmoil.

Having explored the story of the person who caused you pain and having gained insight into their behavior, you are now ready for the next step. For a few minutes, perform a set of heart-opening yoga poses and breathing exercises to align your body, heart, and mind. Then sitting comfortably, close your eyes, center your attention in your heart, and ask yourself this question:

> *What can I do to forgive this person for the pain*
> *I've experienced as a result of their words or actions?*

The emphasis is on what *you* can do, not on what you want or expect the offender to do. You have no control over the other person's choices, and therefore your heart's freedom cannot be dependent upon their actions. To clear the slate, consider what behavior will enable you to let go. Take the energy trapped in the pain and redirect it into a healing and life-supporting action.

Possibilities include writing a letter, burying a memento in the ground, burning a token object that you associate with the person, starting an organization that helps others avoid or recover from similar trespasses, or writing an article or book that documents your experience for the benefit of others. Do something to transform the bad into good, the pain into benefit.

Rachel decided that the best way for her to forgive and move on with her life was to volunteer for a few hours in the Welcome Center of a local Veterans Administration hospital. Interacting with older veterans helped expand her perspective on the challenges her stepfather had faced, allowing understanding, forgiveness, and compassion to awaken within her.

It is not the scale of the action that is important here. The issue is not whether you make a small financial donation or start a new non-profit organization. What is important is that you *do something* that demonstrates your readiness and willingness to forgive and move forward.

Self-Forgiveness

Since you are a human being, the chances are good that sometime during your life, other people have experienced emotional pain as a result of choices you have made. Recognizing your own capacity to act in ways that may have seemed best or necessary at the time, but which caused harm to another, can help you relinquish judgment and awaken forgiveness.

Close your eyes, take a few deep breaths, and settle yourself in your heart. Now bring into your awareness something that you have said or done that clearly generated anguish or distress for someone else. Assessing your situation as objectively as possible, consider the context of your life at the time you engaged in the pain-provoking behavior. What did you do or not do that hurt someone? What were the consequences of your actions? What did you learn from the experience? Without resistance or denial, bring the details of the story into your awareness, noticing the important choices you made that ultimately led to pain for someone else. Take some time now to journal the story, describing what happened, the consequences of your actions, and the feelings that were generated in both the people who were hurt and in you. Once you have fully documented your sin of commission or omission, close your eyes again, settle your awareness into your heart, and ask yourself this question:

What am I prepared to do to enable me to forgive myself
for my actions that caused pain to another person?

It is not uncommon for people to be more willing to forgive others than they are to forgive themselves. Self-recrimination, remorse, and regret may be helpful for a time to focus your attention on behaviors that had hurtful consequences, but life is too short to carry the pain indefinitely. At a certain point, the guilt becomes a trap that inhibits one's ability to use the lesson to any beneficial effect.

Self-pity can be a mask for self-importance, with guilt and remorse keeping people from embracing healing and love in their lives. For example, I recently consulted with a woman named Cary, who was suffering from insomnia. She told me that she lay awake at night blaming herself for her elderly mother's death in a nursing home. She had been unable to care for her mom in her house because her own arthritis made it difficult to provide the physical support her mother needed. A devout Christian, Cary believed that her mother was in heaven, so I asked if she thought her mother had forgiven her. She unhesitatingly replied, "Of course." I then asked her if she thought God had forgiven her, and she affirmed her belief in a forgiving Creator. When I pointed out that she was more demanding of herself than either her departed mother or God, she recognized that it was time to reengage in life, which is what her loving mother would have wanted for her.

Doing Our Best

Life is for learning, and evolutionary growth depends upon trial and error. The poet Maya Angelou has said, "We do the best we can with what we know, and when we know better, we do better."

Through your experience, you are now in a position to commit to a new course of action that demonstrates your willingness to accept responsibility for your anguish-creating actions and your preparedness to do things differently.

Consciously making amends for something that we know caused pain, helps rebalance the scales of life, allowing the past to be past and the future to unfold. Consider what an appropriate penance might be for you to get on with your life. Perhaps it is writing a letter asking for forgiveness, volunteering to work at a charitable organization, or making a donation to a cause that is related to your indiscretion.

I repeat, life is for learning. With the awareness that your choices may have had unintended consequences, take this opportunity to mark the event and set the intention for emotional freedom.

Confession Frees the Heart

For this step, you will once again need a listening partner, someone you can trust with your story of something you did that caused pain for another person. As before, ask your partner to listen to you without interrupting. Share what you are committed to doing to generate restitution for your offense. When you are finished, ask your partner to say these three sentences to you:

I am sorry for the pain you caused.

I'm sure you were doing your best from your level of consciousness at the time.

Assuming you honor your commitment to make amends, you deserve to be forgiven.

During workshops, I ask participants to confess their story to several different people, until they are tired of telling it and the emotional charge has been dissipated. The process usually requires several repetitions, so see if you can share your story with at least three different people you trust. Each time, make your pledge to do something that demonstrates your commitment to repair the damage (to the extent possible), and ask each person to say the same words to you as above.

Envisioning Forgiveness

If you do not have a partner with whom you feel safe sharing your story, you can employ visualization to achieve a similar benefit. Sit comfortably, close your eyes, take a deep breath, and envision yourself in a place of safety and natural beauty such as a mountain ridge overlooking a lush valley or a warm tropical beach.

In your sacred place, envision a being of love and compassion sitting beneath a powerful tree of wisdom. Your being may be a religious figure, a wise man or woman, or a celestial being of light.

Just as you would express your story to a human being sitting next to you, confess to this sacred archetype the episodes that caused pain. With your eyes closed, share your story, as if you were with this being in person.

After sharing your story, imagine your inner healer saying these three statements:

I am sorry for the pain you caused.

I'm sure you were doing your best from your level of consciousness at the time.

Assuming you honor your commitment to make amends,
you deserve to be forgiven.

After you have told the story several times, sit alone and quiet your mind through meditation. Now tell the story to yourself for the final time, as honestly as possible. Having forgiven yourself for the acts you've committed that caused pain to others, make the decision to forgive others for the pain they have caused you. When you fully recognize that the stories you tell determine the quality of your life, you are free to love.

Up in Smoke

I introduced you earlier to the Ayurvedic principle of agni, which is the inner fire that enables us to digest the events of our life. When the fire of transformation is doing its job of metabolizing what is happening to us, we transform the experience into something that either nourishes us or teaches us. A healthy fire generates heat and light, leaving only fine ash as residue. A weak fire, on the other hand, fails to fully transform the raw material of our experiences, generating smoke and leaving behind charred remains.

The next step in the healing process is a ritual based on the transformative power of agni. You will need a safe place where you can light a fire, such as an outdoor fire pit or an indoor fireplace. As a demonstration of your commitment to transform the experiences of the past, take your list of painful memories and toxic traits (the sutras you created earlier). Add to it a few words that represent the personal indiscretion, transgression, or impropriety you just identified. Once you have completed your list, start a fire and burn the list, offering it to the transformational flames of agni. At our Chopra Center workshops, we build a campfire and invite each participant to release their inventory of painful experiences and traits into the fire. Then we roast marshmallows and make "smores" with chocolate and graham crackers. The symbolism is simple: We have the capacity – *you* have the capacity – to transform sorrow into sweetness.

Step to Freedom

Honor your commitment to settle all quarrels with others and with yourself. The anger, hostility, and resentment you believe you are directing to another only hurts your own heart. Nelson Mandela reminds us, "Resentment is like drinking poison and then hoping it will kill your enemies." Do what needs to be done to bring peace to your heart and to those you love.

The Ritual Is Important

I was recently approached by a man who admitted he had been feeling resentful towards me. A woman he'd been seeing on and off for years had attended one of our workshops at the Chopra Center, and she was no longer willing to engage in their emotionally turbulent relationship. For months his anger had been festering, disturbing his peace. When I asked him how I could help, he told me that just being heard was healing for him.

My lesson in this exchange was experiencing firsthand how the person who harbors hatred, resentment, or hostility suffers exponentially more than the one to whom these negative feelings are directed. I was not even aware of this man's anguish and yet subconsciously he believed that his anger was hurting me.

It's important to emphasize that while we cannot afford the luxury of resentment, we also cannot make a mood of forgiveness; that is, we cannot say we have forgiven until we authentically feel compassion and freedom when we look into our heart. It's common to hear people say that they believe forgiveness is important and so they have decided to forgive their abusive parent, betraying spouse, offensive boss, and so on. In many cases, they are simply putting the bandage of forgiveness over a smoldering wound. They may push painful feelings out of awareness, but this provides only partial, temporary relief. In Ayurvedic terms, repressed feelings are emotional ama, which contributes to imbalance and, ultimately, disease in the mind-body system. To truly experience the emotional release and healing of forgiveness, you need to do the emotional clearing work first.

Many people I've worked with have expressed doubts about their ability to forgive. They wonder if they will ever be able to let go. Be assured that complete and natural forgiveness is accessible to every heart, for it is the nature of life to eliminate toxicity. Given the opportunity, your heart will release the uncomfortable feelings generated from boundary-violating, need-denying experiences, but you must create a safe space for this process to unfold.

Moving from Constriction to Expansion

Forgiveness expands our heart. Insults and injuries, whether emotional or physical, tend to move us into a constricted or contracted state. At a primitive level this contraction has a protective intention. In the same way that a person being beaten curls into a fetal position in the effort to protect against life-threatening blows, we emotionally contract to protect ourselves from further wounding. Unfortunately, this defensive response also locks in the pain. For genuine healing to occur, a safe environment must be established so that defensive reactions become unnecessary and unproductive. Then we can do the work of identifying, mobilizing, and releasing emotional pain, which allows authentic healing and transformation to occur. The step of forgiveness closes the chapter on the past so that a new story, rich in love, happiness, and creativity, can be written.

Courageous Action

I cannot overemphasize the important of taking an action step that demonstrates your commitment to forgive another and to forgive yourself for choices that generated pain. In the Jewish faith, the most High Holy Day is Yom Kippur or the Day of Atonement, when observant Jews review the past year, ask for divine forgiveness, and commit to making better choices in the coming year. There is a phrase in the prayer book that says, "For sins against God, the Day of Atonement atones, but for sins against another human being, the atonement does not occur until an effort at reconciliation and forgiveness has been made." Since our ultimate goal is to experience a state of *at-one-ment,* two of the most courageous actions we can take are to ask a person we have hurt for their forgiveness and to offer our forgiveness to someone who has caused us pain. Forgiving another person for something they did to cause you pain and asking for forgiveness from someone you hurt are equally essential acts of healing.

It takes tremendous courage to see someone in a new light that reflects your more expanded understanding of life and love, but the risk has unbounded potential for expanding your freedom to love. If you can create the opportunity, I encourage you to invite your tyrant or victim to a healing exchange. Go for a walk, tell your story, ask for their forgiveness (if you are responsible for the pain) or offer your forgiveness if you were wounded. You may or may not get the response you are seeking (even to the invitation), but in your self-referred state of being, you embrace the wisdom that you can control your choices, though not their consequences. By surrendering your attachment to a particular outcome, you will either feel better or learn something of value through this exercise.

In formulating your intention, consider that the ultimate goal is to allow both of you to have a more open heart. If you can get to the point of being able to say, "Thank you for what you have given to me; I wish you the best on your life's journey; I release you with love," you will experience a new level of exhilaration.

The Talmudic sage Rabbi Eliezer taught that we should fully make amends for our indiscretions on the day before our death. When his student pointed out that few people can know with certainty that they will die the next day, he replied, "Then, just in case, it might be a good idea to fully atone today." This is the advice of a man who understood the value and power of having a heart that is free to love.

*

Through the sacred work you have completed, you have released the emergency brake on your heart that has been limiting your capacity for love and healing. You are now ready to decide where and how you wish to move forward, creating a mind and body that expresses and celebrates your new insights and understandings. In the next couple of chapters, we will look at how we react to the people in our lives and how we can respond more consciously to create the love we deserve.

Chapter Eight

From Healing to Awakening

Those who see themselves in all beings live in peace.

— CHANDOGYA UPANISHAD

As I observe people along their life path, I look for evidence of a transitional point beyond which they move from healing to awakening. Healing from our past is an essential aspect of expanding our sense of self and awakening our capacity to love. This shift often manifests as a change in the questions we've been asking ourselves. Instead of *What do I need?* we ask, *How can I serve?* Instead of *What am I getting out of this?* we start to ask, *What can I bring to this situation to promote the highest possible outcome for everyone involved?*

Awakening into love is a lifelong path. We begin as innocent beings, fully dependent upon our caregivers for all our needs, without a clear sense of separation. As we grow up and become adults, most of us learn to see the world in terms of "us" and "them." We see ourselves through the limited eyes of our ego, which believes it is separate from everything and must fight for its survival. The ego defines "good" as anything that fulfills its needs and supports its views, and "bad" as anything that seems to threaten its existence. However, each of us has the capacity to transcend this dualistic perspective in which differences fuel conflict. We can learn to embrace the inherent paradox of life, which accepts the coexistence of opposing values without needing to negate one for the other to exist. The wisdom traditions call upon us to remove the blinders that prevent us from experiencing ourselves as expressions of the One becoming the many. From this state of being, all manifestations are understood as demonstrations of spirit, and therefore of our essential self. It then becomes impossible to harm others because they are simply our Self in other disguises.

This state of unbounded awareness goes by many names. Buddhists call it *nirvana,* and Hindus refer to it as *moksha.* In Christianity it is known as *grace. Yoga, enlightenment,* and *satori* are other names for the experience of pure consciousness. It is living simultaneously on both the individual and the universal levels. Most people have glimpsed this timeless, infinite space when they are in love. Even as they carry out their day-to-day responsibilities, their awareness of their beloved is omnipresent. In the state of union, even as we perform our ordinary responsibilities, awareness of our essential sacred nature is never lost.

The mind thrives on duality and polarity, while the heart seeks reconciliation and the embrace of contradictions. The ego mind says *no*; the heart says *yes.* If we can look below the surface of any situation, circumstance, belief, or thing, we will discover the seeds of its opposite. In the recognition that something "bad" or "wrong" can produce something of value, we move towards wholeness.

Finding Light in the Darkness

Reality is a selective act of perception. Two people observing the same event will have different experiences, as they filter the energy and information through their personal history and needs. Cultivating flexibility in your perceptions of others and yourself plays a vital role in attaining emotional freedom and physical healing. In the next exercise, you will practice the art of seeing your stories from a different point of view.

Return to your list of undesirable traits you identified in Chapter Four. Perhaps your list looks like the following:

1) Overly sensitive
2) Unattractive
3) Lazy
4) Critical
5) Procrastinator
6) Closed-off
7) Selfish

Looking at your list, see if you can reframe each negative quality in a way that allows for something positive to emerge. For example, you might take the term *overly sensitive* and reframe it as, *I am connected to my feelings and those of others.* Look for a way to see each trait in a different light that allows for healing and transformation. Here are more examples:

Negative Trait	Reframed
Overly sensitive	Connected to my feelings
Unattractive	Not obsessed with appearance
Lazy	Easygoing
Critical	Discriminating
Procrastinator	Cautious before proceeding
Closed-off	Careful
Selfish	Self-reliant

Reframing each negative trait allows you to be less judgmental and more accepting of your humanity. The purpose of this exercise is not to deny that we all have traits that could benefit from improvement, but to see how our judgments embolden and magnify a negative characteristic. When you can shift your perspective of a core belief, you free yourself from its imprisoning influence and are in a much better position to make the changes you are seeking in your life. It is easy to focus on an inherited or acquired quality or trait and believe that this characteristic is the cause of your discontent.

The path to awakening requires embracing your strengths and vulnerabilities without overly dramatizing your perceived imperfections. There is a difference between taking yourself too seriously and taking responsibility for your choices. The former seldom leads to the expansion of emotional freedom, while the latter makes it inevitable. Recognizing that we have a choice allows us to consciously direct our attention to interpretations that are healing, empowering, and liberating.

The evolutionary impulse carries us from separation to unity, from fragmentation to wholeness – or as Jungian psychologist Robert Johnson describes it, from struggling with contradiction to embracing the paradox. The word that best conveys this enticement to wholeness is *love*.

The Essence of Love

In English we use the word *love* in a wide variety of contexts. A child loves her teddy bear. A teenager loves a pop star. A young man loves his new car. A husband loves his wife. A mother loves her child. A disciple loves his guru. This single word expresses our feelings in so many different situations because love is the connection that expands our sense of self. Love bonds the part with the whole, uniting the individual with the universal. We use this common expression differently in different ways depending upon our stage of life and sense of self, but in every case, the essence of love is the pull to unity.

Love is the experience of returning to wholeness. When our physical body is our primary identity – when we think *I am my body* – we seek union through physical contact. Parents embracing their children, friends giving each other hugs, and lovers entangling their bodies reflect the physical expression of love, for touching blurs the boundaries between self and other. In that moment of embrace, individuals are unified and their sense of self expands.

When my oldest daughter, Sara, was about three years old, she would awaken almost every night and climb into our bed. I was aware of various approaches to helping children sleep soundly, ranging from the family bed approach (everybody sleeps together) to strict controls. I asked a doctor friend of mine, a neonatologist, what his thoughts were about keeping kids in their own bed, and he said to me, "It's funny that most single adults I know spend the majority of their waking time trying to find someone to sleep with, yet we expect babies to sleep by themselves." Our bodies fulfill their need for connection by touching other bodies.

When we experience the world from an emotional perspective, we seek unity through revelation and resonance. We hope to be accepted for who we are, seeking out others who share and reinforce our view of ourselves and the world. When we first meet someone, we show them a facet of our persona – a mask that we want them to see. If they respond in the manner we anticipate, we are encouraged to show them another side. In this way, we progressively reveal ourselves, hoping that we will be acknowledged and appreciated. The people with whom we feel the greatest intimacy are those who love us because of, and in spite of, who we are. We feel safe sharing any aspect of our being without fear of judgment or rejection. The ability to recognize and embrace the full range of human qualities within ourselves expands our capacity for creativity and compassion. Integrating the hidden dimensions of our nature brings peace and wholeness, and is therefore a crucial element of healing and awakening.

Finding the Hidden Self

In the early twentieth century, psychiatrist Carl Jung introduced the concept of the shadow self, which refers to all those parts of ourselves that we have rejected and buried in the unconscious. As we are growing up, each of us develops a shadow self that holds all of the qualities that we've learned are undesirable or unacceptable in our family and culture. Common shadow traits include greed, neediness, selfishness, insecurity, and jealousy. Most of the time, we keep these traits hidden, out of the fear that they will sabotage our ability to meet our needs. However, when we can safely reveal our dark forces without fear of losing the love we need, our heart expands. This emotional expression of love unites our individuality with another's.

Each of us has the capacity for unconditional love. Most personal love is like a laser beam focused on one object of attention to the exclusion of others. Personal love usually has an underlying bartering quality – I give something to you for something in return. Higher love is the expression of an expanded sense of self.

Evolutionary Expressions of Emotional Needs

Most of us did not receive formal instructions on how to love. We learned by observing our parents, siblings, and caregivers, who may or may not have been competent at managing and demonstrating their emotions. Judging from my personal and professional experiences, most people have a fairly undeveloped emotional skill set.

If we succumb to unconscious emotional patterns, we demonstrate the primitive love skills we learned, and the same patterns are repeated generation after generation. We can trace our emotional inheritance back to the original dysfunctional family of Adam and Eve – and we know from the Bible how their children turned out.

As a consequence of our childhood dependency on our parents, we tend to model ourselves after them. If yours, like so many, were emotional amateurs, you likely have experienced challenges in meeting your love needs as an adult. Although people spend countless hours in therapy and counseling, seeking to figure out *why* they are who they are, having an intellectual understanding of why you are anxious or unhappy may not translate into feeling better. To create emotionally nurturing relationships, you need to learn new, more effective ways to experience and communicate your feelings.

By becoming more conscious of the principles and patterns that drive emotional responses, you can learn to recognize and express your feelings in healthier ways, expanding your sense of self and your repertoire of responses. The fruit of this effort is wholeness, freedom, better health, and more nourishing relationships.

Bringing Awareness to Emotions

Emotions are physical sensations associated with thoughts in your mind. They are the essential mind-body experience. How you identify yourself, what you are thinking, and ultimately how you feel determines the priorities and choices you make from moment to moment. Your choices reinforce your view of yourself and others, while your emotions provide the signals that alert you when your sense of self is being challenged or reinforced.

For some people, their identity and self-image are closely tied to their physical body. Their highest priorities may be working out at the fitness club, having a fashionable hairstyle, wearing stylish clothing, or following what they believe is the best diet. Any perceived threat to their sense of physical identity (someone criticizes the way they look, for example) generates discomfort. Other people may primarily identify themselves in terms of their role, job title, position, or career. Their attention is focused on achieving the goals they have set for themselves. If they perceive a threat to their role, such as the potential loss of a job, being passed over for a promotion, or losing a case, their mind-body system produces feelings of distress. For others, their identity is based predominantly on their set of beliefs. They feel discomfort when their core tenets appear to be under fire (for instance, if someone disparages their religion or political views).

What you decide is *yours* (e.g., your diet, your style, your position, your view on abortion) determines what you feel you need to defend. Threats that challenge the boundaries of your identity generate sensations that attract your attention. As we discussed in Chapter Five, these sensations are our emotions or feelings.

At the most fundamental level, we have the capacity for only two basic feelings – those of *comfort* and those of *discomfort*. Emotions are the messages your body sends to your mind from your boundaries of self-identity. When something or someone makes contact with your skin, which is the boundary of your physical self, nerve fibers send you a message of either comfort (a loving caress) or discomfort (stepping on a tack). In a similar way, as your emotional boundaries are approached, you receive signals of comfort (someone compliments you) or discomfort (someone criticizes you.) A signal of comfort usually encourages you to move towards the source of stimulation, while a signal of discomfort persuades you to move away from it. We can express these poles of emotions in different ways:

Comfort	Discomfort
Pleasure	Pain
Happiness	Sadness
Love	Fear
Relief	Distress

Whether or not you are consciously aware of it, every decision you make is based upon the expectation that your choice will generate more comfort, or at least less discomfort. This is true whether you are choosing a partner, a job, or a brand of toothpaste. You may be willing to endure short-term discomfort with the expectation that the longer-term payoff will be worth it, as when you step up your fitness routine to lose those love handles, or cram for an exam because you want to go to graduate school. But in the end, it is the expectation of greater comfort, pleasure, or happiness that drives all of our choices.

Although every one of us is driven by this pleasure/pain principle, that which generates comfort or discomfort is different for each person. If you like strawberry shortcake, eating it for dessert will bring you pleasure. On the other hand, if you are allergic to strawberries, the same experience will generate feelings of distress. Some people thrive on the exhilaration of a roller coaster while others wouldn't take a ride even if they were paid.

To begin bringing our unconscious emotional patterns into conscious awareness, we need to ask ourselves a critical question:

What determines whether I interpret an experience
as comfortable or uncomfortable?

When I ask this question at seminars, invariably the first answer is "prior experiences." It is, of course, true that past experiences influence our responses. If you were taken care of by a nurturing, Hungarian nanny when you were a child, you learned to associate her accent with kindness. As an adult, when you meet people from Hungary, you are predisposed to anticipate kindness from them. On the other hand, if you had childhood piano lessons with a harsh, demanding, abusive teacher from Hungary, hearing someone speak with that familiar accent might elicit anxiety in you today.

While past experiences influence our present perceptions, we do not have to be slaves to our conditioning or emotional Pavlovian dogs. We can go beyond our habitual thought patterns and make new life-supporting choices. An ancient Vedic expression declares, "The wise use memories, but do not allow memories to use them." As human beings, we have the gift of free will. It is our decision whether or not to unwrap the present.

Needs: The Heart of Emotions

Here is the question again: *What determines whether we interpret an experience as comfortable or uncomfortable?* If past experience is not the whole story, we have to look to the present, which means that we have to listen to our body. Remember, emotions are sensations in the body associated with thoughts in the mind. From the perspective of our body, our feelings of comfort or discomfort are primitive. We feel comfort, happiness, and pleasure when we are getting our needs met. We feel distress, sadness, and pain when we are not. *All emotions derive from needs. All emotions derive from needs.* Repeat it to yourself like a mantra until you grasp the simple profundity of this insight. When you do, you will possess a vital healing tool: the ability to nurture your emotional well-being. Whenever you are uncomfortable, in distress, or in emotional pain, you can begin to change your situation by realizing that you are suffering because you are not getting something you need (or want).

We can observe these core emotional principles in action by watching young children. When a child wants to be held by his mother, being picked up makes him happy; not being held makes him sad. On the other hand, when the child wants to play with his friends, being held makes him miserable, whereas running free brings him pleasure. Emotions derive from needs. When our needs are being met, we feel comfortable. When they are not, we feel uncomfortable.

If you can accept that needs determine emotions, you are ready for the next step: recognizing and communicating your needs more consciously. Experiencing greater emotional well-being flows from mastering the ability to clearly communicate what you want in life. This is a learned response. If you are not currently adept in this area, it is because you learned from people who were not proficient. Now is the time to improve your skills.

Why We Are Disappointed

If I need something from you, but you do not provide it to me, there are three possible explanations. The first is that you are incapable of meeting my needs. If I want you to train for a marathon with me, but you have a torn meniscus in your knee, you are unable to meet my needs.

The second possible reason you are not meeting my needs is that your needs are in conflict with my needs. For example, if I *need* your help drying the dishes, but you *need* to pay bills, uncomfortable feelings born of our conflicting needs may be activated. In this situation, we can learn to skillfully negotiate so that both parties experience benefit from the interaction. In every circumstance there is a best-possible scenario in which the needs of both parties are at least partially met.

The third and most common reason you are not meeting my needs is that I have not done a good job of clearly communicating what it is I require from you. When we master this skill, we find that people we previously considered incapable or reluctant become both competent and willing. The better we become at communicating our needs, the more likely we are to get our needs met.

Reactions to Needs

Healthy boundaries are required for life to thrive and evolve. Boundary violations disperse energy and disrupt equilibrium. When boundary threats or disruptions occur, we react to repair the breach. The response we choose depends upon the threat and upon which aspect of our identity is threatened. Understanding these responses enables us to make more conscious choices to meet our needs.

Protecting the Body

When the integrity of our physical body is threatened, we activate a vigorous physiological reaction known as the "fight-or-flight response." This primitive response evolved thousands of years ago to help us meet our biological need to acquire food without becoming somebody else's food. The fight-or-flight response redirects all available energy to ensure physical survival. Here is what happens in the body when this response is triggered:

Response	Purpose
The blood pressure rises and the heart rate accelerates . . .	Increasing the delivery of sugar and oxygen to tissues
Stress hormones are released from the adrenal glands . . .	Increasing the intensity of mental and physical activity
A shift in hormones raises the blood sugar level . . .	Delivering more energy to the muscles
Blood is redirected from the digestive organs to muscles . . .	Enabling you to run faster or fight harder
Cortisol release suppresses the immune system . . .	Redirecting life energy to immediate survival needs
Blood-clotting platelets become stickier . . .	Slowing blood loss in the event of an injury

In the face of eminent physical danger, the fight-or-flight response can be lifesaving; however, the body's tendency to activate this response when the threat is more psychological than physical contributes to many of the health challenges we face in modern society. Hypertension, coronary heart disease, anxiety, addictive behaviors, irritable bowel syndrome, obesity, and even cancer have their roots in the fight-or-flight response. When we feel threatened – even by something as small as an unreturned phone call or a critical remark – the body still gears up for a stressful event. As numerous studies have found, chronic stress accelerates aging and makes us more vulnerable to serious illness.

For those rare instances when we need to run for our lives, there is value in having this response in our repertoire. In the past, throwing rocks or spears at our adversaries may have kept us safe, but now that our weapons have apocalyptic capabilities, we must evolve beyond this primitive response for our personal and collective well-being.

Protecting the Ego

According to Ayurveda, just as we have a physical body, we have a subtle or emotional body. We form this subtle body through our attachments to people, positions, possessions, and ideas. To create a physical body, we wrap our DNA with food. To create a subtle body, we wrap our soul with our attachments and aversions. Just as we wear clothing both to adorn and buffer our physical body, we wear our positions and possessions to adorn and buffer our emotional body.

The constellation of relationships and things over which we declare ownership constitutes our ego mind or self-image. The average person has an enormous number of attachments – many of which are at an unconscious level. To gain insight into some of your own attachments, imagine that you've invited new friends to your home and you are getting to know each other better. How do you describe yourself? What do you talk about? What do you share? Do you have favorite stories that you like to tell? Do you tend to identify yourself with a particular political party? A sports team? A hobby? Your career? Your role as a parent? As you show your friends around your house, what are you particularly proud of? Your organic garden? Your designer couch? Your books or wine collection? Your children's photos? Alternatively, what things do you feel the need to apologize for? The mess in your backyard? That your dog needs grooming? The size of your kitchen? By playing through this scenario in your mind, you can begin to see some of the ways in which you currently define yourself.

Consider the numerous things over which you can declare ownership by filling in the blank after the words *This is my*_____. Consider your answers for a few moments. A short list may look like the following:

This is my . . .

> spouse.
>
> house.
>
> child.
>
> job.
>
> car.
>
> religion.
>
> diet.

Your attachment to these people, things, and beliefs makes you feel vulnerable when they fail to meet your expectation or when your sense of ownership is challenged. When someone or something fails to meet your expectations or challenges your sense of ownership, you may react in a habitual way. For example, if you spend the day at the shopping mall finding the perfect dress for a party, and your partner criticizes your choice, his response crosses your "mine field," triggering a reaction. If you spend the day refinishing a piece of furniture and your partner does not find your work professional, the violation of your ego boundary has the potential to upset you.

Our responses to subtle-body infringements are thinly disguised fight-or-flight reactions. We usually don't hit a person who crosses our ego line; rather, we say something hurtful so that the offender retreats. Sarcasm, criticism, and name-calling are psychological forms of the *fight* response. The purpose of these attacks is to reestablish an ego boundary that has been breached. Using information someone has told us in confidence is a particularly powerful stealth weapon.

Emotional withdrawal and shutting down are the psychological disguises of the *flight* response. Pouting, withholding affection, not responding to calls, and refusing to give attention are emotional equivalents of physically running away. Pulling back is the ego's effort to protect itself from a perceived threat by restoring its boundaries.

Honing Our Emotional Skill Set

To get our ego needs met, we experiment with different psychological approaches. The Yaqui sorcerer Don Juan told anthropologist and apprentice Carlos Castaneda that human beings use four primary mechanisms to reinforce their self-image: being nice, being nasty, being indifferent, or assuming a "poor me" stance.

For example, my seven-year-old, Izzy, sees a doll in a toy-store window and employs her "nice" need-meeting response, asking, "Daddy, will you please buy me that doll?" If I do not succumb to her charm, she transitions to her "nasty approach," crying and demanding I fulfill her desire. If this tactic doesn't yield the desired response, she may go into a indifferent or withdrawn mode, refusing to talk to me. And if this method fails, she might try her wounded "poor me" response, telling me, "You always buy Sara (her older sister) what she wants. You must love her more than me." Even at her young age, Izzy has become quite proficient in her repertoire of techniques designed to meet her needs.

We each have our own inventory of psychological tools we use to cajole, manipulate, seduce, threaten, and control other people in our efforts to meet our needs. The patterns we develop are usually established in early childhood, a time when these tools may have been our best hope. Throwing a tantrum may have actually worked when you were five years old. Hiding in your closet may have attracted the attention you were seeking. The challenge now is to recognize that these primitive responses may no longer be meeting your needs. Fortunately, we have the capacity to develop new ones.

Step to Freedom

Notice throughout the day every time you feel the impulse to activate the fight-or-flight response. Become conscious of the underlying principle of boundary violation or unmet need that triggers the urge to lash out or withdraw. Don't attempt to willfully change your responses. Simply witness your reactions so that you can become intimate with the tendencies that drive your response patterns. As you become mindful of these inclinations, you will feel less controlled by them.

From Ego Mind to Witnessing Awareness

Going beyond the layers of our physical and subtle bodies, we can identify the core needs that drive all other needs: the need to feel happy, the need to feel love, the need for good health, and the need for meaning and purpose in life. To enable these higher-level needs of the soul to drive our choices, we must quiet the mind through the regular practice of meditation.

Over the years, studies of meditators have shown that just as we have a tendency to react aggressively when our self-image or body is threatened, we also have the capacity to return to a balanced mind-body state. During meditation, mental turbulence quiets and the body enters a deep level of relaxation. The heart rate and breathing slow, stress hormone levels are reduced, and the immune system is strengthened. The quiet centeredness we experience in meditation begins to permeate our daily life, enabling us to make the choices that have the greatest likelihood of generating the outcomes we seek.

From the platform of inner stillness, we begin to take ourselves less seriously, while behaving more responsibly. Seriousness usually reflects self-absorption, born from a sense of victimization and the fear of boundary trespasses. Responsibility flows from the recognition that we are co-creators of our life and that most of what happens to us is the consequence of our choices.

We have both the capacity to activate a war response that requires us to expend energy in defense, and the capacity for a peace response that replenishes our life energy.

War Response *Fight or Flight*	Peace Response *Meditation*
↑ Heart rate	↓ Heart rate
↑ Blood pressure	↓ Blood pressure
↑ Respiration	↓ Respiration
↑ Perspiration	↓ Perspiration
↑ Stress hormones	↓ Stress hormones
↓ Anti-aging hormones	↑ Anti-aging hormones
↑ Platelet stickiness	↓ Platelet stickiness

As we recognize our ability to self-regulate our physical and emotional states, we become less dependent upon and less reactive to the situations and circumstances swirling around us. We become intimate with a state of quiet awareness, and our sense of self starts to shift. We begin taking furloughs from the prison of an ego-restricted identity and experience ourselves as an expression of nature. Established in this state of being, our sense of self expands, along with our capacity to love.

When we move from a state of constriction to expansion, we begin to see love not as a sentiment or emotion, but as a practice that benefits both the lover and the beloved. In the next chapter we will refine this practice for becoming mindful, masterful lovers, radiating love in every intention, thought, word, and action.

Chapter Nine

The Practice of Love

Please bring your heart near me.
For all I care about
Is quenching your thirst for freedom!
All a Sane man can ever care about
Is giving Love!

— HAFIZ

LIBERATED FROM THE INNER DIALOGUE THAT REINFORCES SELF-PITY
and self-importance, you are now ready to create love in your life. This
requires mastering the skill of identifying and communicating your
expectations and needs in ways that maximize the possibility of getting them met. At the same time, cultivating love is an inner journey.
Through the regular practice of quieting and centering yourself, you
connect to your true nature, which is whole, perfect, and abundant in
love. Established in this awareness, you know that even when you don't
get exactly what you want, you are comfortable and fulfilled. This is
the great paradox of love – the better you are at generating a state of
internally created peace, the less you are dependent upon others to help
you feel good about yourself. And the less needy you are for others to

make you feel whole, the more appealing you become, and the easier it is to attract love. People who know themselves as lovable easily draw others into their lives who are willing and happy to love them. Knowing that you and those in your life are inherently deserving of love, you can develop the skills of identifying and communicating what is needed in order to make your relationships more loving.

Conscious Communication

In his book *Nonviolent Communication,* psychologist Marshall Rosenberg reminds us that how we communicate our needs plays a major role in our ability to get them met. If you have the mind-set that you're a victim of the situations, circumstances, and people around you, you will feel powerless to direct the course of your life. By contrast, if you have the attitude that you are the co-creator of your experiences, you will focus on creating conditions that are likely to increase the chances of getting your needs met.

The better we become at meeting our needs, the greater emotional well-being we experience. Emotional turbulence arises when outcomes do not align with our intentions – when our experiences do not fulfill our expectations. As we've seen, this emotional upset can be viewed as a response to an unmet need or to someone crossing our boundaries without our permission. How we react to the unmet need or boundary violation determines how long and to what extent we remain emotionally imbalanced. Our goal is to regain emotional balance or freedom, wasting as little energy and time in turmoil as possible. To this end, we need to be conscious of how thoughts in our mind generate sensations in our body and then employ new strategies to quiet mental turbulence and regain emotional balance.

From Past to Present

The first step in subduing emotional distress is identifying what happened to disturb your peace. This requires staying in the present and resisting the tendency to layer this current upsetting situation with emotional debris from your past. Here are a few familiar examples to reinforce the point:

You phone your wife, who tells you that she is in the middle of a meeting and will call you back in fifteen minutes. An hour transpires and your call has not been returned, so you call her back, angrily declaring, "You never make me a priority in your life!"

You are listening to your favorite talk show host on the car radio while you are waiting to pick up your partner at work. Your partner gets into the car and promptly changes the radio station. You become furious and say, "You are so controlling. You act as if you're the only one who ever deserves to get their way!"

Your husband leaves for work at six in the morning and returns home at 11 p.m. You meet him at the door with a bitter accusation. "You care more about your job than you do about your family!"

As you begin to pay attention, you will notice how readily you inject your past into your present. The first step in creating emotional freedom is to stop doing this. This requires consciously asking yourself, *What happened?* and not indulging in conditioned dialogues rooted in the past. It's a skill that requires practice, for the mind has a natural tendency to draw upon memories and view the present through the lens of past experiences. This ability to stay "in the now" develops through the regular practice of meditation, in which we learn to redirect thoughts from past ruminations and future anticipations to present moment awareness.

Continuing with the examples above, let's separate the facts of the situation – what actually happened – from our interpretation based on past conditioning.

What Happened?	Interpretation based on Past Conditioning
My spouse didn't return my call within one hour.	I'm not their highest priority; I'm not that important to my spouse.
My partner changed the radio station.	My partner is a control freak who doesn't care about what I want.
My husband left for work at 6 a.m. and returned at 11 p.m.	My husband cares more about his work than our family.

When we contaminate our present with conditioning from the past, there is a high probability that the current situation will unfold predictably. Our goal is to enliven unpredictability, for creativity is being able to bring forth something new, to have a different response that opens up greater possibilities for love and intimacy in our relationships. We seek new ways to communicate our needs so that we have a better chance of getting them met.

From "You Make Me Feel . . . " to "I Am Responsible"

The language we use to communicate our feelings creates the reality of our experience. Time and again, I see how people's fears of what might happen almost ensure the dreaded outcome. For example, a manufacturer's representative is so anxious about a customer finding other sources for their products that she drives away the very business she is trying to maintain. A jealous husband is so controlling that his partner leaves out of a feeling of suffocation. A woman, who withholds her affection out of fear of being vulnerable, loses her partner to a more demonstrative woman.

The conscious wording of our feelings can move us forward to getting our needs met. Certain words used to describe feelings are inherently victimizing and are best avoided in thought and speech. Here is a sampling of words I encourage you **to eliminate** from your vocabulary, which includes your self-talk, for they declare to yourself and the world that you have surrendered responsibility for your feelings to others:

Abused	Abandoned	Betrayed
Controlled	Cheated	Deceived
Duped	Exploited	Humiliated
Intimidated	Manipulated	Neglected
Rejected	Suckered	Taken advantage of

Of course, people *do* abuse, abandon, betray, and neglect others. This is undeniable. However, if your goal is emotional freedom, it's counterproductive to reinforce a victim stance by replaying, over and over, mental dialogues such as *I feel abused, I feel abandoned, I feel neglected,* and other self-defeating messages.

Victimization language does not describe feelings; rather, it is an assignment of intention. Saying "I feel rejected" implies that the other person's intention was to reject you. It's difficult enough to be sure of our own intentions! Your accuracy in defining someone else's is therefore suspect. So instead of giving another person authority over your internal state, use language that reflects your willingness to assume responsibility over your emotions. Instead of saying you feel *abandoned,* say you feel *lonely.* Instead of *rejected,* use the word *unimportant.* Here are more suggestions for translating victimizing language into words that demonstrate your willingness to assume responsibility for your emotions:

Abused	→	Powerless
Betrayed	→	Naïve
Cheated	→	Foolish
Exploited	→	Empty
Manipulated	→	Defenseless
Neglected	→	Invisible

I am not suggesting that you deny uncomfortable feelings that arise when your boundaries are crossed or your needs are not met. What I'm saying is that the language you use to communicate your feelings will have a substantial impact on your ability to change them.

From "Figure It Out" to "This Is What I'm Asking from You"

As babies and young children, we are aware of the discomfort we feel in our bodies as the result of a need before we are aware of the need itself. A baby's cry may mean hunger, tiredness, or a call for affection, and it is Mother's job to decipher the message and then recognize and fulfill the need. As we mature, we generally become better skilled at identifying and communicating our needs, but most relationships falter because, at a deeper level, we still want the other person to figure it out for us. A psychologist friend of mine says that most relationships fail because one or both of the people involved expect the other to psychically read their mind. She calls this *E.S. Peeing* on your partner. In reality, *you* are the best person to identify and communicate what you need. Fortunately, even though people spend an extraordinary amount of energy making their emotional needs seem complex, they are usually pretty basic:

- *Attention* – the sense that you are important to me and that, therefore, I am willing to make you (at times) the object of my full focus.

- *Affection* – the connection that comes from loving physical contact.

- *Appreciation* – the sense that I value you for your contribution to me.

- *Acceptance* – the acknowledgment that I recognize that you are the best you can be at every moment, while allowing you the space to grow into your full potential.

The key principle of conscious communication is making it as easy as possible for the other person to meet your need by asking for the specific behavior that will fulfill it. However, when people feel vulnerable, they commonly compensate by becoming demanding and threatening, believing that forcefulness will increase the likelihood of getting what they want. As often as not, this approach has the opposite effect. My demand of you implies that you are of lesser value than I am and that, therefore, I have the right to dictate to you. Even if you give in to my belligerent demands, you will likely do so with resistance and resentment. Sooner or later, you will no longer be willing to acquiesce to my commands and will stop meeting my needs. Although we want to help our loved ones get their needs met, when they make demands, we feel imposed upon. If you are a parent, you probably attempt to convert your children's demands into requests on a regular basis. When you tell them, "Say please, " or "What is the polite way to ask for that?" you are teaching them to reframe their need in a way that elevates rather than denigrates your self-esteem.

Mastering Conscious Communication

The way you express your needs is one of the most conditioned aspects of your personality. You learned it by observing your parents and it became your style, whether or not it was consistently effective. People often become attached to what is most familiar to them, even if it is has not been proven to be the most successful. When people who grew up in different cultures or environments come together to get their needs met, they approach the relationship with different (internalized) rules of engagement. Then, as they play the game of love, infractions are inevitable, for what was fair on one playing field is foul on another. If you are to create peaceful relationships, it is essential that you agree to express your needs in ways that have the highest probability of serving both you and the other person, and to play by rules that both of you agree are fair. To see how this works, let's look at a few common scenarios.

Scenario #1

You go to a party given by friends of your new partner. You are standing alone while your partner is engaged in lively conversation with an acquaintance.

Conditioned Response:

"I saw you flirting with that person and I feel betrayed by you. If you do this again, don't expect me to ever come to another party with you."

Conscious Response:
"When I saw you talking with that person, I felt invisible. I need to feel at ease when I go with you to a place where I don't know anyone. Will you please introduce me to some of your friends so I can feel comfortable while you are talking with other people?"

Scenario #2

Your partner went food shopping and did not purchase the type of breakfast cereal you eat each morning.

Conditioned Response:
"You never think of me when you go shopping. I'm tired of you taking advantage of me. I'm going to stop doing all the things I do for you since you never reciprocate."

Conscious Response:
"I ran out of my favorite cereal and was hoping you would have noticed and bought it for me. I would appreciate it if you would ask me what I need when you make a grocery store run. Can you please do this for me?"

Scenario #3

You arrive home from work and find your spouse and children playing video games in the family room. There are dishes in the sink and clothing items on the floor.

Conditioned Response:

"I'm sick of being the only one to clean up around here. Everyone treats me like the maid! I feel completely unsupported by this family and I'm tired of exhausting myself so you can play video games."

Conscious Response:

"I've been working all day and arrive home to see dishes in the sink and laundry on the floor. I'd really appreciate some help from you to maintain some orderliness in this house. Can everyone please pitch in for the next fifteen minutes and clean up the house while I start dinner?"

In each scenario, the conditioned response has two consistent elements: (1) The speaker applies past experiences to the present, so that the historical pattern dominates the immediate event; and (2) The speaker has an expectation that others already know what they need and are, therefore, intentionally withholding the behavior. There is an underlying sense of victimization that says, in essence, "You know what I need and are purposely refusing to give it to me."

In contrast, a conscious response deals with the present experience as an independent event. The need is not assumed to be obvious and therefore the person takes on the responsibility of identifying the need and communicating the behavior that will meet it.

This critical skill set can transform any relationship. I encourage you to master it by practicing the following simple method. Here are the four steps:

1) Whenever you feel upset, realize that it is because you have an unmet need.

2) Identify what happened that was different from what you expected.

3) Identify what you need that you did not get.

4) Ask for the behavior, being as specific as possible.

Although using this process does not guarantee that you will always get your needs met, it will increase the probability that you will spend more time feeling comfortable and less time in emotional distress.

As you become adept at conscious communication you will become increasingly confident of your ability to get your needs met *to the extent possible* given those elements that are within and outside of your control. Conscious communication is a skill that gets better with practice.

Recapitulation

Having exerted the effort to release emotional toxicity from the past, you are now in a position to consciously avoid accumulating emotional ama as you move forward. Recapitulation, the technique of reviewing your choices and experiences at the end of each day, is a valuable technology for enhancing your communication skill set and keeping your heart free from toxicity. Practiced regularly, it will enable you to avoid falling back into old emotional patterns.

Recapitulation is best performed at the very end of the day, after you have completed your evening routine, turned out the lights, and are ready to sleep. Begin by placing a pillow behind your back and, sitting comfortably in bed, close your eyes and meditate for five to ten minutes, using a mantra or following your breath. Once you feel settled, begin reviewing your day from the moment you awoke in the morning. As if you are watching a video on the screen of your awareness, notice the events and interactions that unfolded throughout the day. Pay particular attention when your body generates feelings of comfort and discomfort. Noticing which situations still have an emotional charge provides clues that you may need to pay more attention. See if there is something left undone from the day.

You may notice while recapitulating that you were abrupt with someone because you were preoccupied. You may notice that you failed to give one of your children the attention they were seeking. You may have forgotten to return someone's call. If you identify anything "left over" from the day, make a commitment to complete it the next day. Apologize to the person to whom you may have been rude; pay extra attention to your child; return your friend's call.

Don't permit emotional ama to accumulate in your heart. When you no longer harbor resentment, grievance, or regret, you will be available to experience and celebrate all of the gifts available to you in this moment. Behind the curtain of self-pity and self-importance, love and knowingness patiently await.

Step to Freedom

For the next seven days, practice recapitulation just before you go to sleep. Spend five to ten minutes reviewing your experiences and responses throughout the day while attending to the feelings in your heart and body. If any discomfort arises as a result of noticing that you may not have been as open-hearted as you would like, make a few notes in your bedside journal so that you may rectify the transgression the next day. Observe how this simple heart-clearing technique influences your relationship with yourself and those around you.

Commit to Compassion

People are transformed by love. The very nature of love expands our sense of self and our capacity to treat others tenderly. The distinctions and differences that separate and divide us from others become less attractive than what unites us. Personal love becomes less personal as our internal identity becomes less constricted. Maharishi Mahesh Yogi used to say, "All love is directed to the Self. I love you, but it's no concern of yours."

We move from personal love to higher love by adding silence to our awareness. While we are engaged in our inner dialogue about what has happened in the past or what we anticipate in the future, we remain imprisoned in our personality, limited by the stories we tell ourselves. When we are able to quiet our thought traffic through meditation, we glimpse the expansive state between our thoughts and recognize that we are much more than we think we are.

Adding silence to love raises us up. As we recognize that all beings are the same Being in disguise, we move from personal love to compassion. This is the essence of Spiritual love. The brilliant, and at times controversial, guru Rajneesh (now known as Osho) used to say that love on a physical level is expressed through sexuality and reflects our animal nature. Love on an emotional level is expressed through relationships and reflects our human nature. Love on a spiritual level is expressed through compassion and reflects our divine nature. Our divinity is that which celebrates our existence, independent of our positions and possessions, our accomplishment and achievements, our acquisitions and experiences. When we can live in this state of grace, we become authentic lovers in all of our relationships.

Perform this simple exercise to see how easily you can temporarily shed your usual personality trappings and still be you.

Sit comfortably, close your eyes, and take a few slow, deep breaths. Bring your attention to your environment and consider everything around you over which you declare ownership by assigning the value "my" or "mine." You might think, *I have my house, my car, my job, my spouse, my kids, my plasma TV, my favorite football team.* Now let go of all these people, positions, and things.

Next, bring your attention to your body and become aware of the sense of ownership you declare over your body. *This is my hair, my gut, my diabetes, my heart.* Now let go of your body.

Become aware of your breath. Notice the inflow and outflow of your breathing, which continues whether or not you are paying attention. Hold your breath in full inhalation and notice how uncomfortable you feel when you resist releasing, even though it is time to let go. Now hold your breath in full exhalation, noticing the discomfort you feel when you resist receiving, even though it is time to accept. Now let go of your breath.

Bring your attention to your mind, noticing the arising and fading of thought forms. Watch the thoughts of the past and future come and go, like waves on the ocean of your awareness. Now let go of your mind and simply sit in the presence of your own being. Notice that your inner state of wholeness is independent of your positions and possessions, independent even of your body and mind.

As you emerge from this quiet, expanded state, bring into your awareness the people with whom you have important relationships. Imagine loving them from this place of expansion, without need or expectation. Envision that with your now more open heart, you can accept the people in your life as they are, with all their attractive and distasteful qualities. Your expanding inner wholeness enlivens your ability to love unconditionally.

The experience of love is healing. Premature babies touched lovingly develop faster. Love enhances immune function, improves digestion, lowers blood pressure and can even reduce cholesterol levels. Patients who believe their doctors and nurses genuinely care about them recover faster than those who don't. Love awakens the innate healing power of our mind and body.

Love is an ability that improves with practice. Every drop of love is sacred. Every impulse of love moves us in the direction of unity. Now that you have invested your time and attention in removing the obstacles to an open heart, commit from this point forward to making love, in all of its expressions, the most important thing in your life.

Chapter Ten

Writing a Great Love Story

Ever since Happiness heard your name,
It's been running through the streets
Trying to find you.
— Hafiz

Congratulations on reaching this point! Assuming you didn't skip the previous nine chapters and have performed the exercises, you are not the same person you were when you picked up this book. You have identified emotional residue from your past and brought it into your conscious awareness, where you have separated the emotional charge from the facts of the experience. Through the recognition that people are doing their best from their level of awareness, you have substantially relinquished feelings of regret, resentment, and guilt, replacing them with understanding and forgiveness. You are committed to practicing conscious communication so that you can approach your relationships with the skills to identify and convey your needs in ways that enhance the likelihood that they will be met.

The question now is, *What story do you want to see unfold from this point forward?* You have the opportunity and responsibility to create an authentic life, one in which you are the writer, director, and lead actor, rather than a bit player in someone else's tale. Everyone enjoys an epic story, which is why we tell them over and over. Look what's playing now at your local movie theater. Most storylines are either about good triumphing over evil, or love prevailing over estrangement. A heroic figure, despite all odds, is able to overcome destructive forces and re-establish justice, fairness, and harmony in the world. Lovers who are pulled apart find their way back into each other's hearts. These are the perennial tales that we have been telling each other since the beginning of humankind.

Falling in Love with Your Self

You are powerful, intelligent, and interesting. You are complicated and valuable. You are attractive. You are a good person. You are worthy of love. You are deserving of happiness.

My hope is that you can embrace these truths more readily now than when you started this book. Say them to yourself and see if you can embody the essence of this recognition without real or feigned modesty, without self-pity or self-importance.

You have these lovable qualities and more because you are living the gift of a human incarnation and have this rare opportunity to be a conscious manifestation of the universe. Your individuality is a wave on the ocean of universality. Even as each wave expresses its unique qualities and talents, it retains its essential oceanic nature. To use another metaphor, gold can be made into bracelets, charms, and coins, but its elemental goldenness cannot be destroyed.

You are the universe playing hide-and-seek with itself. You are the sacred in disguise. You are God in drag. Knowing this, you cannot feel sorry for yourself for very long, because your heart and soul retain the memory of your essential divinity. With this awareness, you have the capacity to create a compelling life story – a story in which you are free to love and in which you love freely.

Your inner being is perpetually seeking to seduce you. Although it faces stiff competition from the sensory enticements of the world, your soul is not a jealous lover. Connect with it regularly and it will gladly share you with the world. Through the clearing of emotional confusion and misunderstandings, you have taken a major step towards embracing your true nature. The more clearly you recognize who you really are, the easier it is to see through all of God's other disguises. Then, no matter where you are or whom you're with, you will feel comfortable and open, because you know at your core that you are divinity expressing itself in a living form – as are all the other sentient creatures you encounter in life. Living and loving from the center of your being, you are always at home with yourself.

Be Kind to Yourself

When you love something, be it a puppy, your garden, or a child, you naturally want to take good care of it. Now that you are committed to choices that support and reinforce your happiness, treat yourself with the same intention and caring you'd give to anything else you love. Minimize toxicity; maximize nourishment. Life-damaging habits, which in the past provided temporary relief from your sense of unlovability, have outlived their usefulness. You no longer need to anesthetize yourself from yourself. Look at your use of love-substituting behaviors and begin trusting your internal pharmacy of well-being, rather than depending upon chemicals that temporarily modulate your emotions. Commit to a regular practice of meditation, yoga, exercise, and conscious communication, and enjoy the power you have to create balance from within, reducing your need for outer acts of manipulation.

Look at every aspect of your life and identify experiences that are depleting rather than nourishing. Evaluate your food, water, air, music, TV, internet sites, and job choices and see how you can reduce the ingestion of energy and information that is not serving you, while replacing it with that which does.

As you are making your commitments to be more nurturing to yourself, it is essential that you make conscious choices about your relationships. As you know by now, relationship toxicity can be as or even more harmful to your psychological and physical health as a poor diet, excessive alcohol, or recreational drugs. And, sometimes freeing yourself from a toxic relationship can be more difficult than letting go of a toxic substance. It takes courage and sobriety to become disentangled from associations that are boundary violating or energy depleting.

People remain in toxic situations primarily out of fear – fear that they will lose financial security; fear of being judged harshly by family, their religious community, or God; fear that they will irreversibly harm their children; and fear that they will not find anyone else to love them. If you are currently in such a relationship, your highest and healthiest self must take the lead in guiding you to freedom. Each of your fears must be addressed directly, for it is impossible to love freely or heal yourself if your life is dominated by fear. Seek advice from a trustworthy financial expert, solicit the support of family and clergy, realize that you are not serving your children if their household is perpetually turbulent or strained, and draw upon your closest friends whom you trust only want you to be happy.

It has been my experience that people who identify, mobilize, and release emotional toxicity from the past find it nearly impossible to tolerate a relationship that offers little emotional nourishment. If you feel stuck in a relationship that is creating ongoing pain for you, begin healing it or start planning your exit strategy now. Using your creativity, timing, and finesse, you can be free to love again.

The Most Important Relationship

People often find the motivation to engage in emotional healing when a relationship ends. The pain and loneliness of going from being a couple to being single provide a powerful incentive for looking at oneself and one's patterns. Although it may not feel like it at the time, being in-between relationships can be an incredible gift. I encourage you to take full advantage of this opportunity to recreate a state of lovingness that transcends the need for a lover.

The most important step if you have recently come out of a painful relationship is straightforward, though not always easy: *wait*. If you immediately jump into a new love without taking the time to find your center and heal your heart, you are almost guaranteed to perpetuate the turmoil. Take time to fall in love with yourself. As a rough rule of thumb, take one to two months for every year of your last relationship before you even consider starting a new one. Spend this time with yourself and with supportive family and friends until feelings of desperation subside. They will. Not until you are genuinely comfortable spending time with yourself are you in a position to begin engaging with another person.

Be particularly alert to people who want to rescue you from your broken heart. Rescuers are attracted to vulnerable people who help them feel important and needed. The problem is that once you start feeling stronger, many rescuers become insecure and transform into petty tyrants. They need for you to feel weak in order for them to feel strong, so if no one else is creating pain for you, they assume the role.

When you are hurting, someone who wants to make you "all better" is understandably attractive but often delays the healing process. Be open to relationships with those who support and trust your healing process but do not attempt to fix you.

Pay Attention

Every aspect of our being is present in seed form. When you are ready to find love, recognize that all potential patterns of a relationship are broadcasting their promise from the moment you begin exchanging energy and information. It's natural when you fall under the spell of love to see those aspects that reinforce your ideal and ignore those that do not. Everyone has light and dark elements, and most of us have become good at disguising those characteristics that we'd prefer others not see.

Still, the heart sees it all. Under the influence of love, your mind, noticing a behavior that's less than appealing, will use its power to deny. *He doesn't really drink that much. She's really not that obsessed with material things. I'm sure his flirting will end once we're fully committed to each other.* These are the common denials that often become terminal issues in relationships.

It's natural to hope that the enthusiasm you experience in the early stages of a relationship will compensate for any potential disagreements down the road. People do shift their behavior for their own or another's benefit, but an important question to ask yourself when you notice a pattern is, *Can I live with this behavior if it persists?* If your willingness to create a deeper bond is predicated on the expectation that you can "fix" someone, take a few steps back before diving in too deep. Now that you have brought the light of healing into your heart, you do not need to look to someone else to make you whole because you now know that wholeness is your inherent state.

Creating Enlightened Relationships

For many of us, relationships offer the greatest challenge to emotional freedom. Almost everyone would like to experience peace and harmony with the people in their lives but often struggle to manifest these desires. Most people envision an ideal intimate relationship based upon shared interests, open communication, mutual nurturing, and passion. Because many have been unable to create this level of emotional connection, they determine that they need to "work" harder to create the love they seek. People often tell me they are seeking a "serious" relationship, but it has been my experience that lighthearted ones are generally more desirable and longer lasting.

A person struggling in an established relationship often complains, "I've come to realize that we are two completely different people." This is an important realization, for if people believe they are the same person in two different bodies, they are likely to be disappointed. Successful relationships accept that no two individuals have exactly the same needs, expectations, beliefs, or tendencies. Finding common ground while honoring differences in perceptions and perspectives is the basis of healthy connections.

Although there is no proven formula that applies to all relationships, embracing a few key principles in your heart will reduce conflict and enhance the flow of love. These principles are valuable in friendships and business relationships, as well as in families, marriages, and intimate partnerships.

1) My relationships are based on equality.

Relationships based upon inequality may survive but will never thrive. Love is the unity that comes from seeing yourself in another and the other in you. Despite inevitable differences in financial productivity, educational background, physical beauty, or IQ, your deep and unassailable self-talk must be, *I am not above you or beneath you. We are different expressions of the same underlying being and, as such, are of equal value.* You may have heard of the Sanskrit greeting *namaste*. The essence of this expression is, "The spirit in me recognizes the spirit in you and knows them to be one." In day-to-day exchanges, namaste translates as a willingness to see the other person's point of view and to recognize its validity even though you may not share their perspective.

2) My relationships are mirrors of myself.

If there is discord in a relationship, ask yourself how you may be contributing to the conflict. Before blaming the other person for what they are or are not doing, search your heart and see what you might be able to think, say, or do differently to shift the dynamics. If you are seeking more attention, can you be more attentive? If you are seeking more affection, can you be more affectionate? If you are seeking more appreciation, can you be more appreciative? If you are looking for greater acceptance, can you be more accepting?

It is considerably more challenging to change another person than it is to change yourself (and that's not easy either!). Seeing others as mirrors of yourself empowers you to change someone over whom you have control (you), rather than becoming frustrated with your inability to change someone else. The real secret is that when you transform yourself, the world around you cannot help but change.

3) My relationships have room for change.

Life is inherently dynamic. Everything is continuously changing, including your thoughts, feelings, and molecules. We all seek some constancy in the midst of change. We often are attracted to a relationship for the stability it offers, but too much stability can sow the seeds for conflict. It's common for people to say, "You're not the person I married," or "You're not the same person you were when I first met you." Although this is usually hurled as an accusation, it is a statement of reality. Everyone is carried along by the river of change, and two people will not necessarily change in the same way at the same pace. The door to change only opens from the inside.

Accept that change is a part of life. Evolution calls upon us to adapt to change with creativity. Look for ways your relationship can accommodate and celebrate the inevitable changes that life serves up, while seeking to maintain the connection and commitment that transcends the field of change.

4) In my relationships, I let the past be past.

In every relationship, people experience conflicts or difficulties that leave a residue of resentment, hurt, or disappointment. These remnants of past battles are often used as armaments in the next argument. *You did this! You didn't do that!* Carrying the past into the present escalates the conflict but rarely helps us get our needs met. Make a commitment to not bring up past transgressions when dealing with a current issue. Reopening old wounds during a disagreement or argument seldom supports healing, reconciliation, or transformation. Practice recapitulation on a regular basis and allow each day to unfold unencumbered by remains of the past.

5) In my relationships, I choose being happy over being right.

If you engage in a win-lose orientation, there will be times when you experience the fleeting exhilaration of winning an argument, as well as the temporary frustration or embarrassment of losing. However, neither winning nor losing translates into loving. People disagree because they believe that their point of view is correct – or at least better than another perspective – and it's rare that someone changes an entrenched position as a result of vigorous debate. On the contrary, the more emotional effort we expend in reinforcing our viewpoint, the more likely the other person will dig in their heels.

The alternative is to look beyond the obvious differences and seek common ground. People move into defensive positions when they feel that their point of view is being disparaged. See if you can take a small step in the direction of the other person's position and ask for a similar level of compromise. Interrupt the pattern of conflict by acknowledging your differences while seeking creative solutions that can enable both of you to get your needs met.

6) I nurture my relationships through the power of attention, affection, and time.

Whatever we put our attention on grows stronger in our lives. Therefore, if you want a relationship to flourish, you must be willing to nurture it with your time and attention. As we discussed in Chapter Nine, many disagreements and emotional reactions have their roots in the unmet basic needs for attention and affection. Arguments about how much time a partner spends at work can be resolved with a loving hug and an unhurried conversation. Just listening attentively can be nurturing. This means consciously committing not to respond until the other person has completed their thought and you've taken at least a few moments to digest the information. Reacting before you've allowed the other person to express themselves fully moves you toward a situation where both people are speaking (and at times escalating into shouting) at the same time without anyone being heard.

We also demonstrate our attention through body language. A few moments of eye contact and a direct facing posture declares, "You are worthy of my attention. You are of value to me." The power of attention cannot be underestimated. It is like fertilizer to relationships, whether the object of attention is a baby, your pet, your partner, or your friend. As a doctor, I am repeatedly reminded of the healing power of attention.

Loving Touch

Physical affection also provides essential nourishment to relationships. Studies on the healing power of touch remind us how necessary it is for healthy human development. Premature babies who are regularly touched develop faster and leave their incubators sooner than babies who are not. Children with HIV infection show immune stabilization if they are hugged regularly. Loving touch releases a shower of natural pain-relieving and mood-elevating chemicals throughout the body.

Touch is the most direct means we have to close the gap between separation and union. Technology enables us to see and hear each other from a distance, but cannot create the essential connection and fulfillment that comes from touching. Affection lowers the volume on mind chatter and promotes feelings of safety, comfort, and relaxation. In short, loving touch is good for your body, heart, and soul, so be generous with your affection.

We demonstrate our priorities by the amount of time we are willing to invest. For relationships to flourish, they must have time allocated to them. I have repeatedly found that one of the most effective interventions I can offer for a floundering relationship is to suggest that the couple go away for a weekend together. When partners are able to re-experience each other as loving human beings rather than merely as defined roles (my husband, my wife, my business partner), the original passion that began the relationship can often be rekindled.

7) In my relationships, I am prepared to communicate my expectations and negotiate the price.

Relationships developed millions of years ago because they provide evolutionary benefits. Subatomic particles "decided" it was in their best interest to congregate as atoms. Atoms determined they could benefit by sharing electrons and uniting as molecules. Single cells took a leap of faith when they came together as multi-cellular communities – just as we do when we make a commitment to a relationship. We act in faith with the expectation that our lives will be enhanced by moving from "I" to "we."

There is a price to pay for surrendering your autonomy. Committing your attention implies that there will be other areas of interest that you will not be able to explore. It means that there will be times where you don't get all that you want in a given situation in exchange for getting more of what you want in other situations. Your skill in negotiating what you're prepared to give and what you expect in return determines the success or failure of your relationships. The more consciously you can identify and communicate your expectations, the more likely you are to create a healthy, evolving bond. If your heart is generating signals of discomfort because you are not receiving a good return on your emotional investment, ask yourself what you need that you're not getting. Then, express your needs in ways that maximize the probability of getting them met. This includes hearing what the other person requires and being willing to negotiate win-win solutions. These principles apply whether you are seeking to heal an existing relationship or intending to create a new one.

Love Is a Practice

Cultivating your lovability – your ability to love and to be loved – is a lifelong pursuit. You now have the basic skills to play the game of love with finesse, but do not imagine that you can master it, for love will challenge you throughout your life.

Commit to the power of love. Don't allow the accumulation of toxic emotions that constrict your heart. Instead, use the tools of emotional clearing and keep your sights on the loving being you can and deserve to be. Listen to the wisdom of your heart and allow it to guide you into higher expressions of love.

If you believe it, you will create it. Whatever conditioning you received growing up about your lovability, you are now in the position of knowing at your core that you deserve love. Any belief other than this is false and should find no sanctuary in your heart. Ralph Waldo Emerson wrote, "What you are shouts so loudly in my ears, I cannot hear what you are saying." By now you know that what you are is divinity disguised as humanity. As such, love is your essence and will be your dance partner for life.

Chapter Eleven

Living in Love

This sky where we live
Is no place to lose your wings
So love, love, love.

— HAFIZ

IN CHAPTER 1, I ASKED YOU TO COMPLETE A QUESTIONNAIRE THAT assessed your emotional state. Now that you have read the book and (hopefully) have completed the exercises, I again ask you to take this inventory of your current emotional condition. Please complete it as honestly as you can, using the following scale:

0 = almost never
1 = rarely
2 = occasionally
3 = frequently
4 = much of the time
5 = almost always

1.	Regardless of what is happening around me, I know I am a lovable person.	
2.	Even when facing significant challenges, I trust I will weather the storm and be okay.	
3.	I care for myself through healthy choices that reflect my intrinsic self-worth.	
4.	I am comfortable spending time alone without feeling lonely.	
5.	I am able to set healthy boundaries with the people in my life.	
6.	I have peaceful relationships with my parents, siblings, and family members.	
7.	I trust my intuitive inner voice, even when others attempt to discourage me.	
8.	I am comfortable with my body image.	
9.	I can handle rejection without questioning my core worthiness.	
10.	I recognize and acknowledge my unique talents and am at ease in expressing them.	
11.	Although at times I may experience episodes of anxiety or sadness, I know that these are passing moods that will resolve.	
12.	I am authentic in my most intimate relationships; I am not leading a "double life."	
13.	I can effectively communicate my needs to those in my life.	
14.	I am passionate and enthusiastic about what I am doing.	
15.	I do not harbor disappointments, grievances, or regrets.	
16.	I am in tune with, and accepting of, my biological appetites and needs.	
17.	I am comfortable giving and receiving affection.	
18.	I enjoy my sexuality without limiting inhibitions.	
19.	I respond to feedback with an openness to improve and without accepting another's perspective as unquestionably accurate.	
20.	I am inherently trusting and trustworthy in my relationships.	
	Total Points	

Compare your current tally to your original score. Having identified, mobilized, and consciously discharged toxic feelings and beliefs from your body, heart, and mind, you will notice a substantial improvement in your lovability score.

In your journal, describe how your life has changed since beginning the *Free to Love* process. What is working for you and in what areas do you still feel challenged? What old patterns have you let go of? Are you now experiencing more spontaneous moments of gratitude and joy? Have you felt empowered to make any changes in your relationships or work? Are you discovering a deeper connection to your spiritual self and purpose? Are you finding it easier to extend compassion to yourself and those around you?

Be gentle with yourself as you reflect on your growth and remember that this planet is a school for the evolution of the soul. If we already knew everything, there would be no reason to attend classes here. By doing the deep emotional healing work in *Free to Love,* you have already completed an advanced course. You have learned valuable lessons from your painful experiences and have broadened your capacity for compassion and humility. The intention now is to continue expanding your sense of self and your capacity to give and receive love in your life.

Loving the One You're With

Imagine that you love someone with every cell in your body. Mothers often feel this way about their baby or young child. Lovers may experience this level of affection in the early stages of their romance when the drug of passion is at its greatest intensity. You may feel this way about a beloved parent who was a constant source of support and encouragement. If you can feel or envision this expansive state of lovingness, you will recognize that it is possible to care for someone so much that your only desire is for that person to be happy.

Now consider how you would feel if you could embrace this level of love for yourself. Although you've probably been taught since before you can remember that while loving and serving others is good, self-love is selfish, I've learned that those people who can genuinely appreciate their own individuality, with all their socially acceptable and unacceptable qualities, are the most capable of genuinely loving and serving others.

If you loved your individuality as much as a mother loves her children, what choices would you make in order to create a life of health, happiness, love, and purpose? You might imagine that, like a devoted mother, you'd want your beloved children to take good care of themselves. You'd hope that they would eat healthy foods, get enough rest, and avoid dangerous situations and substances that could be harmful. You would encourage them to associate with intelligent, creative, and compassionate people. You would encourage them to find their passion in life and develop skills that would allow them to create material abundance while doing those things they enjoy the most. You would want them to have a life rich in abundance, love, purpose, and freedom. These are the experiences we would all like to have, and my hope is that you now believe you deserve them.

Fulfilling the Human Intention

More than five thousand years ago, Ayurveda, the ancient instructional manual of human life, elaborated the four primary human intentions that lead to fulfillment. These are known in Sanskrit as *artha, kama, dharma,* and *moksha.* When you consciously translate these four intentions into choices in your life, each of your days will be filled with new experiences and new understanding. Let's look at each of them.

Artha

Artha means material abundance. On the most basic level, it means having enough food on your table, a roof over your head, and clothing to keep you warm. Many people spend an enormous amount of energy in pursuit of material abundance, only to discover that the goal they've been chasing consumes their life and love. Our current global challenges reflect the artha intention gone awry. In our relentless pursuit to fill our emptiness through acquisition and consumption, we have been depleting our environment's natural resources and heating up our planet. And as consumers became obsessed in biting off more than they could digest, we have collectively contributed to the recent implosion of the world's economies.

An awakened being understands that the essence of abundance does not result from accumulation but from creativity. Knowing that you are an expression of the creative power of nature, you fulfill the intention of artha by nurturing your creativity.

The Vedic tradition of India offers a story about a young man who goes in search of the secret of abundance. After many months of travel through dangerous countryside, he meets a rishi – a spiritual master – and asks him if knows the secret to creating wealth.

The sage pauses and looks deep into the young man's eyes, then says, "Those who seek abundance must choose between two goddesses. The first is the Goddess of Wealth, Lakshmi. She is generous and beautiful and when you worship her, she may, for a time, bestow her treasures upon you. But she is a notoriously fickle master who may capriciously withdraw her support without warning. The other choice is to worship Saraswati, the Goddess of Wisdom. Saraswati wants devotees who authentically seek knowledge, understanding, and artistic delights. If you venerate Saraswati and dedicate yourself to wisdom, Lakshmi will become jealous and try to capture your attention by showering you with wealth and abundance."

As a being of love, you deserve and are capable of creating abundance in ways that enhance your happiness and contribute to the harmony of your community, society, and ecosystem. As more and more people learn to celebrate their innate lovability, our collective need to consume, exploit, and deplete will diminish

Kama

Kama is the intention to create and sustain harmonious relationships, in which the flow of giving and receiving are in equilibrium. Loving beings who are consciously connected to their bodies, hearts, and minds quickly notice when their relationships are moving out of balance and make adjustments to sustain and nurture them.

Too often, I see people desperately attempting to fulfill someone else's needs while neglecting their own. The inevitable consequence is that they become exhausted, resentful or sick. A depleted well cannot quench anyone's thirst. In any relationship, there will be times when you give more, and other times when you receive more. If you or a loved one are going through a difficult situation (such as illness, divorce or loss), the flow of love in one direction may seem disproportionate. In truth, giving and receiving are different forms of the same energy. Still, even if you are in the role of caring for another, recognize that your ability to support someone else depends upon you taking good care of yourself. Relinquish the belief that you must sacrifice your vitality to serve the people in your life. Remember that you serve others best by being grounded, balanced, creative, and abundant.

Now that you know the basic skill set of conscious communication (discussed in Chapter 9), be certain that your heart is open so that you remain in the nourishing flow of love. This means disallowing the accumulation of emotional ama by staying attuned to your own needs and the needs of those in your life.

Dharma

Dharma is the essence of your individuality. As the universal field of pure potentiality manifests as individual expressions, each being is a reflection of the whole and, at that same time, brings something unique to the world. This is the essence of dharma – that everything and everyone has a purpose in life.

Psychiatrist Sigmund Freud said the two most important elements of a healthy life are loving relationships and meaningful work. We can reframe these elements as wholeness and dharma.

One of the most important responsibilities of parents is guiding their children to discover their true dharma. However, even if you did not receive this guidance growing up, you can begin to access the realm of dharma by quieting your inner dialogue and asking your heart two questions: 1) What are my natural talents? and 2) What do I most enjoy doing? If you are seeking clarity about your dharma, take a few minutes after each meditation to ask these questions and listen to your heart's response. As you gain insight into what your heart and soul are longing to express, you will notice that what you're doing to satisfy your own needs also serves those around you.

Moksha

Moksha is freedom. When you analyze any choice you make in your life, you will see that in the end, the intention underlying it is the hope or expectation that you will expand your freedom. Some freedoms take us to a new dimension – the freedom to be happy, the freedom to be creative, the freedom to love. Some freedoms lead us away from bondage – freedom from abusive relationships, freedom from pain, freedom from mundane work. The ultimate freedom that we carry in seed-form deep in our soul is the freedom from a constricted sense of self. Although we spend a lifetime creating and refining an individual personality, our soul remembers that our essential nature is the expression of the infinite. The movement from constriction to expansion generates unparalleled exhilaration.

We move toward freedom within when we quiet our minds in meditation and glimpse the expanded field of awareness that underlies our thoughts, feelings, and choices. We move toward freedom in the outer world when we make choices that are likely to bring us greater joy and lightness of being. Actions that make us feel heavy and deaden our natural enthusiasm bring us closer to the grave. Actions that lighten our hearts bring us closer to enlightenment.

Nurturing Your Body

Our bodies have relatively simple needs. We need nourishing fuel, rejuvenating sleep, and regular activity. Loving parents ensure that their children receive proper nutrition, enough rest, and regular exercise.

Since you are now willing to lovingly care for yourself, this is a good time to consciously fulfill your body's basic needs. Having written hundreds of thousands of words about health, I can now summarize everything I know in a few paragraphs.

Nourishing Food

Long before the United States Department of Agriculture began calculating the Recommended Daily Allowances (RDA) of nutrients, the human body innately knew what it needed to be balanced and healthy.

The ancient healing system of Ayurveda reminds us that our bodies are always trying to tell us what they need to be healthy and vital – including the specific foods we need for our unique mind-body type or dosha. (If you don't know your dosha, you can find out by taking the Dosha Quiz at **www.chopra.com/dosha**).

According to Ayurveda, we can make nutrition simple by ingesting the healthiest sources of six major taste groups: sweet, sour, salty, pungent, bitter, and astringent. If you ensure that throughout the day, you ingest foods from each category, you will maximize your body's potential for health and well-being. Whenever possible, eat food that is fresh and organic while avoiding food that is processed or filled with additives.

Sweet	Grains, pasta, breads, nuts, dairy, oils, sweet fruits, starchy vegetables, fish, poultry, meat, sugar
Sour	Citrus fruits, berries, tomatoes, tart fruits, vinegar, chutneys, salad dressings, pickles, condiments, alcohol
Salty	Table salt, fish, meat, seaweed, soy sauce, processed foods
Pungent	Pepper, cayenne, ginger, garlic, onions, leeks, chilies, radish, salsa, basil, thyme, cloves
Bitter	Green and yellow vegetables, green leafy vegetables
Astringent	Beans, legumes, peas, lentils, tea, cranberries, pomegranates, apples, green leafy vegetables

The second most important component of a healthy diet is listening to your body's signals of hunger and satiety. This means only eating when you are unmistakably hungry and stopping when you are satisfied (but not stuffed.) The easiest way to stay in tune with your need for food is imagining that your appetite is a gauge, where a 1 on the dial means you are famished and 10 means you are completely full. Pay attention to your internal signals and only eat when you're close to empty (level 2) and stop eating when you are at about 70 percent of capacity (level 7). Remember that food is for nutrition. Continuing to eat after the point of satiety overloads the digestive system, resulting in a build-up of toxicity in your physiology. Including all six tastes each day and listening to your appetite are the two essential elements to lovingly nurturing your body.

Appetite Gauge	
10	(stuffed)
9	(uncomfortably full)
8	(overate)
7	(satisfied)
6	(almost satisfied)
5	(no hunger awareness)
4	(could eat)
3	(definitely hungry)
2	(very hungry)
1	(hunger pains)
0	(completely empty)
Eat at level 2. **Stop at level 7.**	

Restful Sleep

It is difficult to be loving if you are tired. In fact, becoming recalcitrant, irritable, or withdrawn are signals our bodies generate when we are fatigued and need rejuvenation. Restful sleep provides the foundation for a healthy body and mind. Here are a few basic suggestions to ensure that you are receiving enough rest.

- Aim to be in your bed with the lights out between 9:30 and 10:30 pm. If you are not used to getting to bed this early, move your bedtime up by half an hour every week, until you are in bed by 10:30.

- About an hour before bedtime, run a hot bath into which you place a few drops of a calming aromatherapy essential oil such as lavender or sandalwood.

- As your bath is running, perform a gentle massage on your head and feet using sesame, almond, or an herbalized oil. You can find full instructions for performing a self-massage at **www.chopra.com/abhy.**

- After your massage, soak in the warm tub for ten to fifteen minutes. Keep the lights low or turn them off and burn a candle.

- As you luxuriate in the water, listen to soothing music.

- After your bath, drink something warm and soothing, such as a cup of warm milk with nutmeg and honey, chamomile tea, or valerian root tea.

- If you mind is very active, journal for a few minutes before bed,

"downloading" your thoughts and concerns so that you don't
need to ruminate about them when you shut your eyes.

- Read inspirational or spiritual literature for a few minutes
  before bed. Avoid dramatic novels or distressing reading
  material.

- Do not watch television or work in bed to avoid activating your
  mind and stirring up thoughts that could keep you awake.

- When you are ready to go to sleep, close your eyes, lie quietly
  on your back, and consciously relax your body – starting by
  bringing your attention to your toes, then moving up your legs
  to your trunk, arms, and head. Notice any area where you are
  holding tension and let it go.

- Then simply observe the slow, easy inhalations and exhalations
  of your breath until you fall asleep.

Move Your Body

Energy flows freely in a healthy body. As we become increasingly
interdependent with technology, it is easy to go through an entire day
without using many more muscles than those responsible for typing on
a keyboard, moving a computer mouse, and pressing a car accelerator
or brake pedal. In the same way that loving parents ensure that their
children get off the computer and out of the house to play, loving yourself
requires a commitment to move your body. Self-loving behavior includes
daily conscious movement to keep your body flexible, strong, and fit.

There are three primary components to a complete fitness routine:
flexibility enhancement, strength building, and cardiovascular conditioning. A regular yoga asana practice can fulfill the first two aspects,

while cardiovascular conditioning requires an aerobic activity that increases your heart and respiratory rate. To receive the greatest benefits from your cardiovascular regimen, most fitness experts recommend that when you exercise, after you warm up, you increase your intensity level until you are breathing hard enough that although you could carry on a normal conversation, you would rather not. At this level, you will also notice a thin layer of sweat on your body. Sustaining this pace for 20 minutes, five times per week, will help your circulatory system function at an optimal level. Combine your cardiovascular conditioning with a daily set of heart-opening yoga poses (instructions are in Chapter 3) and your body will reward you with energy and ease.

Expanding Your Sense of "I"

Every human being has a sense of self. When we are facing a challenge in life, this sense of self tends to be constricted. If you are experiencing discomfort in your body, your world tends to revolve tightly around the symptoms that influence your immediate choices. If you are in the midst of a challenging relationship, your day-to-day reality is focused on the immediate issues that create emotional turbulence for you.

Our sense of self directly affects our capacity for love. When we have a contracted sense of self, we are constricted in our lovability. As our sense of self expands, our ability to love increases proportionately. When we are in distress, our inner conversation revolves around what we need. When we have peace of mind and comfort in the body, our inner dialogue shifts from *What's in it for me?* to *How can I help you?*

Daily Inventory

You now have everything you need to create a life that expands your sense of self and your ability to be a source of compassion for the world.

To support you on your path to wholeness, take a daily inventory of your life by asking yourself these questions of your body, heart, and mind.

Body
- Did I attentively nourish my body today with healthy food?

- Do I feel rested today? Have I taken time to quiet my mind in meditation and did I experience restful sleep last night?

- Have I given my body the opportunity to move consciously today through actions that enhance my flexibility, strength, and endurance?

Heart
- Did I utilize the skills of conscious communication in my relationships today?

- Have I maintained healthy boundaries with the people in my life today?

- Did I take myself less seriously, yet more responsibly, allowing me to engage with others from a more expanded sense of self?

Mind
- Have I set my intentions today with the mind-set that either my desires will be fulfilled or I will learn something of value?

- Have I been open to seeing the world from new perspectives, even those that seem in opposition to my usual point of view?

- Did I learn something new today that expanded my mind and generated enthusiasm?

Free to Love, Free to Live

You have all the ingredients and the recipe to make a magnificent life. Now is the time to mix them together and see what you can create. Choosing a life of freedom is a worthy pursuit that will make every day fascinating, enabling you to live in gratitude. Choosing the path of love will ensure that you always have wonderful beings around you to celebrate your accomplishments and support you during your challenges.

This incarnation is whizzing by at the speed of life, and we don't want to have regrets as we approach the departure gate. As I share the final days with patients who are moving through their transition, time and again they say to me, "It's all about love. It's always been about love. Love is the only thing that's real."

Epilogue

Commitment to Love

When all your desires are distilled
You will cast just two votes:
To love more.
And be happy.

— HAFIZ

FIND A PICTURE OF YOURSELF AS A BABY OR YOUNG CHILD. CONSIDER IT as if you were looking at someone else – perhaps a co-worker's grandchild or a friend's niece or nephew. What do you see? You would probably agree that you are looking at an adorable, innocent new being, ripe with potential and worthy of unconditional love.

Now look into a mirror, gazing into your own eyes. Do you perceive this beautiful being, rich in potential, deserving of unconditional love? You have a lifetime of experiences, some that expanded your heart, and others that were constricting. You have made choices in your life that led to greater happiness and others that created sorrow. Through it all, the essence of your being bears witness to the unfolding of your life, distilling drops of joy and love to nurture your tender heart.

Today is a new day. As an expression of the sacred field of unlimited possibilities, you have the capacity to make this a day filled with love and enthusiasm. Why not live as if it mattered?

My beloved guru, Swami Brahmananda Saraswati, told his students,

This scarce human body is acquired after many lifetimes; don't waste this opportunity. Every moment of life is precious. Do not think of yourself as weak and fallen. That which was done up to now, understand that this was unintentional. But now, apply yourself to action fit for a human.

If having become a human being you do not obtain knowledge of your Divine nature, it is as if you have sold a diamond for the price of spinach.

The world is in need of love. With an open heart, you radiate the light of love to all those around you. Remember, no impulse of love is wasted. As a lover, rejoice in your state of lovingness, and know that every being who reflects a ray of your love is enlightened by the experience. This is your essential state. It always was and always will be.

Do not allow the pervasive worldly demands of life to constrict your heart. The sun does not use the excuse of clouds to stop shining its light, for it knows that clouds will always come and go. It is your birthright to live a life abundant in love. Make the commitment today to open your heart and let your love flow. No matter what has happened in your past, you have an infinite capacity for love. Please use it, for your own sake and the sake of this precious world.

Appendix

Chapter Three

Suggestions for music to accompany your rhythmic breath practice:

MCMXC A.D. by Enigma; Virgin Records, 1992

Unfolding by Axiom of Choice; Narada, 2002

Karma by Delerium; Nettwerk Records, 1997

Tempting the Muse by Mysteria; Intentcity, 2006

To find a certified *Primordial Sound Meditation* (PSM) teacher in your area or to learn more about becoming a certified *Primordial Sound Meditation* teacher, please visit: www.chopra.com/teacher

Chapter Six

Selected References: Scientific Research on the Relationship Between Love, Emotions, and Health

Berk L. (1996). "The laughter-immune connection: new discoveries." *Humor and Health Journal* (5), 1–5.

Case R. B., Moss A. J., et al. (1992). "Living alone after myocardial infarction." *JAMA* (267), 515–519.

Charnetski C.J. Riggers S. and Brennan F.X. (2004). "Effect of petting a dog on immune system function." *Psychological Reports* (95), 1087–91.

Field T.M., Schanberg S.M., et al. (1986). "Tactile/kinesthetic stimulation effects on preterm neonates." *Pediatrics* (77), 654–58.

Ironson G., Fields T., et al. (1996). "Massage therapy is associated with enhancement of the immune system's cytotoxic capacity." *International Journal of Neuroscience* (84) 205–217.

Kiecolt-Glaser J.K., Fisher L., et al: (1987). "Marital quality, marital disruption and immune function." *Psychosomatic Medicine* (49), 13–34.

Kiecolt-Glaser J.K., Stowell J.R., et al. (2005). "Hostile marital interactions, proinflammatory cytokine production and wound healing." *Archives General Psychiatry* (62), 1377–84.

Post S.G. (2005). "Altruism, happiness, and health: It's good to be good." *International Journal of Behavioral Medicine* (12), 66–77.

Spiegel D., Bloom J.R., et al. (1989). "Effect of psychosocial treatment on survival of patients with metastatic breast cancer." *Lancet* (ii), 888–891.

Yoshino S., Fuhimori J., and Kohda M. (1996). "Effects of mirthful laughter on neuroendocrine and immune systems in patients with rheumatoid arthritis." *Journal of Rheumatology* (23), 794–794.

Recommended Reading

Here is a short selection of books that have taught me valuable lessons about love:

Deepak Chopra. *The Path to Love.* New York: Harmony Books, 1997.

Debbie Ford. *The Dark Side of the Light Chasers.* New York: Riverhead Books, 1998.

Jean Houston. *The Search for the Beloved.* New York: Jeremy P. Tarcher, 1987.

Robert Johnson.

　—*He: Understanding Masculine Psychology.* New York: Harper & Row, 1987.

　—*She: Understanding Feminine Psychology,* New York: Harper & Row, 1989.

　—*We: Understanding the Psychology of Romantic Love.* New York: Harper Collins, 1983.

Daniel Ladinsky. *The Subject Tonight Is Love – 60 Wild and Sweet Poems of Hafiz.* Myrtle Beach, South Carolina: Pumpkin House Press, 1996.

Maharishi Mahesh Yogi. *Love and God.* Maharishi International University, 1973.

Marshall M. Rosenberg. *Nonviolent Communication.* Encinitas, California: PuddleDancer Press, 2003.

Shel Silverstein. *The Missing Piece Meets the Big O.* New York: HarperCollins, 1981.

About the Author

DAVID SIMON, M.D. WAS A WORLD-RENOWNED AUTHORITY IN THE field of mind-body medicine. As a board-certified neurologist and expert in Ayurvedic medicine and other traditional healing arts, he brought a unique perspective to the relationship between mind, emotions, and health. In 1996, he co-founded and assumed the role of medical director of the Chopra Center for Wellbeing, where he served as the driving force in developing and leading the Center's programs, workshops, and retreats in mind-body medicine, emotional healing, and spirituality.

Integrating ancient wisdom healing traditions with modern scientific principles, David Simon forged a model of health that integrates the multiple dimensions of a human being – environmental, physical, emotional, psychological, and spiritual. His endeavors resulted in the training of thousands of physicians, nurses, and health care providers.

David was also the author of many popular wellness books, including *Return to Wholeness; The Wisdom of Healing; Vital Energy; The Ten Commitments;* and *Free to Love, Free to Heal.*

About the Chopra Center Press

THIS BOOK IS THE FIRST TREE PLANTED IN OUR NEW GARDEN, THE *Chopra Center Press*. We wanted the experience of cultivating a book from its conception to its release, to ensure that every stage of the process reflected our core intentions of awakening, healing, and transforming the reader. We discovered that with the heartfelt commitment of each member of our team, the final product is more than the sum of its parts.

The enthusiasm and creativity invested by each member of the Chopra Center Press tribe added exponentially to the work. The mission of the Chopra Center for Wellbeing is to serve our global community through the development and offering of authentic knowledge, services, and products that celebrate and support balance, healing, transformation, and the expansion of awareness.

We hope that the reader will sense and appreciate the loving intentions underlying this division of the Chopra Center for Wellbeing. All future offerings of Chopra Center Press will continue to reflect our deepest commitment to serving our global family.

www.chopra.com

The Chopra Center for Wellbeing

THE CHOPRA CENTER FOR WELLBEING IN CARLSBAD, CALIFORNIA, was founded by Deepak Chopra, M.D. and David Simon, M.D. in 1996 to help people experience physical healing, emotional freedom, and expanded awareness.

As the popularity of natural healing practices and mind-body medicine has grown, the Chopra Center continues to serve as the global source for authentic information on meditation, yoga, and Ayurveda. Every year thousands attend the Center's wide range of programs, workshops, and retreats, which include mind-body immersions, emotional healing intensives, and meditation and yoga retreats.

The Chopra Center's Teacher Certification programs are also expanding as like-minded people seek to share the healing gifts of meditation, yoga, and Ayurveda with their communities. Through the global network of Chopra Center-certified instructors, people throughout the world are learning the practical tools for creating balance, peace of mind, and well-being in their lives.

To learn more, please visit www.chopra.com

Experience the *Healing the Heart* workshop

If you are seeking freedom from emotional pain, our *Healing the Heart* workshops will help you access deeper levels of healing. Offered several times each year in the loving, compassionate setting of the Chopra Center for Wellbeing, *Healing the Heart* is a transformative experience led by the Chopra Center's master educators.

You will be guided in the five-step emotional release process, including instruction in meditation, heart-opening yoga, the Seven Laws of Enlightened Relationships, and other powerful tools that you will be able to use to enhance all areas of your life.

Visit **www.chopra.com/healingtheheart** or call **888.736.6893** to learn more.

**Read what past participants say about
the *Healing the Heart* workshop:**

"A truly profound event that opened me up. It has altered my life and perhaps saved it. I am deeply grateful to you and the universe."
~ Karl V., Massachusetts

"This workshop has been the best thing I have ever done for myself. The highlight was releasing my pain, realizing that I wasn't alone, and finding myself. I am so thankful I decided to do this."
~ Sarah B., California

"I needed this safe, nurturing experience where I could be honest and raw. I allowed myself to really feel the pain I was in rather than masking it. I am eternally grateful for this experience."
~ Vivian C., New Jersey

"I have accomplished more healing in the last three days than I have in years of therapy. Working from the inside out is the only way to truly heal!"
~ Jenny L., Colorado

"I feel transformed and empowered and believe that healing is well on its way. The Chopra Center's ability to create a palpable feeling of love and acceptance with a room full of strangers in such a short time speaks to the wonderfulness of everyone here."
~ Craig M., Arizona

"*Healing the Heart* opened my heart and awakened me to a life that I am free to lead. I feel like a cloud has moved away and the sun is shining on me. I am excited to make a difference for myself. I know now that I *deserve* it."
~ Jessica T., California

Index